Praise for Joy o

T0276744

"With *Joy on Demand,* Meng continues to further his goal of promoting a better life grounded in happiness for his fellow human beings. I commend his efforts to build a better world with humor, persistence, and meditation."

—Jimmy Carter, 39th President of the United States

"We live in a world of constant external stimulation where we are told that material success is the source of our happiness and what we have is never, ever enough. In reality, the source for happiness and contentment is within us and can be accessed with one breath. With that, we can experience a natural sense of wonderment and awareness of what is. In *Joy on Demand,* Meng presents mind-training tools such as these that are free of traditional religious trappings and made accessible for everyone. His contagious humor and his gentle guidance have the potential to deeply impact today's society."

—His Holiness the 17th Gyalwang Karmapa, Ogyen Trinley Dorje

"*Joy on Demand* introduces us to a powerful, life-changing idea: No matter where we are in our lives, we all have the ability to access joy. Meng is a wise and entertaining guide, generously sharing his own incredible life story and outlining the practical steps we can all take to actually train ourselves to live life with less stress, more wisdom, and more fulfillment."

—Arianna Huffington, cofounder and editor-in-chief
   of *The Huffington Post*

"What caught my attention was Chade-Meng Tan's confession: 'I started meditating because I was miserable enough to try anything.' So, happiness was not something that came naturally to him; it was a skill he had to learn. But he found that the ability to access joy is highly trainable. Joy led him to success, and now in turn he shows himself to be just the kind of trainer you'd hope for: he answers your questions exactly when you are about to ask them as you read along. He is not talking *at* you, but *with* you and shows compassion even for the laziest cats among us. Meng is fun to be with and fun to read. Fun, even when he writes about serious concerns. Let's be honest: what concerns us more seriously than how to be happy? But he knows that it is equally important to also learn working with pain as we train ourselves in the art of joy. Yes, in *Joy on Demand* Chade-Meng Tan proves to be a brilliantly convincing salesman for the power of joy. Yet, he does more than persuade: through step-by-step exercises he *delivers* the goods."

—Brother David Steindl-Rast, OSB, cofounder
    of A Network for Grateful Living

"Sometimes the most simple ideas are the hardest to grasp. Using his meditation training, Chade-Meng Tan shows how we can reliably access the vast and transcendent nature of joy and transform it into a sustainable resource that increases the happiness in our everyday lives."

—Sakyong Mipham, author of *The Shambhala Principle*

"*Joy on Demand* reminds us that we all have a seed of joy inside of us. This book will tickle that special place in you that will ignite more happiness in your heart."

—Goldie Hawn, Academy Award–winning actress,
    producer, and bestselling author

"*Joy on Demand* is a formidable articulation of what it means to cultivate mindfulness in all its dimensionalities, and why it is worth persevering with both effort and effortlessness. Meng's logic and clarity are inspiring, infectious, and transformative."

—Jon Kabat-Zinn, founder of Mindfulness-Based Stress
    Reduction (MBSR) and author of *Full Catastrophe
    Living* and *Coming to Our Senses*

"This wonderful book is fun to read, with cartoons, jokes, and banter all along the way. But don't let Meng's humor and lightheartedness fool you into thinking his ideas are just funny too. As many who have long practiced meditation can attest, including Meng himself, the instructions given in *Joy on Demand* can transform your life. Enjoy the book and train your mind! You'll be happier for it."

—Sharon Salzberg, author of *Lovingkindness* and *Real Happiness*

"A wonderful how-to book on the joys of joy and the way to get there. Chade-Meng Tan, the Jolly Good Fellow at Google for years, takes readers on a lightning path through his own discovery, via meditation and science, of the deep and high value of joy. He should know: he is an engineer, and a very funny one at that. I loved reading his book. It is full of smiles, questions, cartoons, and stories, plus a lot of good science, that make it a very rich read. *Joy on Demand* is a treasure house of the heart and mind."

—Roshi Joan Halifax, Ph.D., abbot of Upaya Zen Center

"Chade-Meng Tan seduces you with taking the first step, which is paying attention to one breath. And, if going beyond that is too boring or difficult, do it again. Which means you have now paid attention to the second breath. A Zen master asked: How long is one lifetime? Answer: A lifetime is the period between two breaths (meaning the first and the last). *Joy on Demand* is a title that is half meant in humor, but only half. It is a serious introduction to meditation, the more profound for it being so simply explained. I am now on my next breath."

—George Yeo, chairman of Kerry Logistics and chancellor
    of Nalanda University

"This book DEMANDs your enJOYment."

—Tony Hsieh, CEO of Zappos.com

"In this book, Meng helped me to see that joy isn't just an emotion; it's also an action. By tapping into the joy that is deep inside all of us, we gain access to the foundational building blocks of creating a happy life."

—Chip Conley, bestselling author of *Emotional Equations*
    and hospitality entrepreneur

"Meng has captured the subject of our search for joy with his usual elegance and humility. With both great respect for teachers and their wisdom, and simple reductions to the essence of the work, he gives us all a path to follow that is clear and calm. All one must bring is the intention for a more joyful and resilient way to live, and these pages will do the rest!"

—Scott Kriens, chairman of Juniper Networks
    and director of 1440 Foundation

"This is an important book written by a visionary who has become one of the world's foremost advocates for finding joy at work. Chade-Meng Tan is a rare breed—someone who understands the research but can make these ideas practical and usable even in a fast-paced world. His friendly style makes you feel like you're sitting down for coffee at Google with him right before he teaches his famous mind-training course. Tan has found a way to make meditation and joy the bedrock principles of one of the most successful companies in history by articulating their value through humor and wisdom. *Joy on Demand* will definitely help you find greater joy and success in your work as well."

—Shawn Achor, happiness researcher and bestselling
author of *The Happiness Advantage*

"When a book offers practical, scientific insights on success and happiness, I'm intrigued. When that book also has cartoons, I'm in. Meng's book is a joyful look at where we can find more joy in our lives."

—Adam Grant, professor at the Wharton School and *New York Times* bestselling author of *Give and Take* and *Originals*

"With Meng's new book, joy is about to go viral. These simple, delightful instructions make it as easy to experience—and share—as it could possibly be."

—Steve Chen, cofounder of YouTube

"We humans are privileged to have access to a higher kind of joy than other animals—joy that comes from doing good, being kind, having a sense of humor, creating music, and finding peace of mind. With *Joy on Demand*, Meng reminds us that this human joy is the most reliable, lasting, and truly joyful kind and shows us how to use nothing more (or less) than our own human minds to get it."

—Ray Kurzweil, inventor, author, and futurist

"Unlike many books, *Joy on Demand* delivers on the promise of its title. Let Meng teach you the simple yet powerful skill of meditation—and happiness and success can be a mere breath away. Along with joy, you'll find calm, clarity, and creativity through discipline of the mind. What do you have to lose?"

—Dan Pink, bestselling author of *To Sell Is Human* and *Drive*

JOY
ON
DEMAND

The Art of Discovering the Happiness Within

CHADE-MENG TAN

Illustrations by Colin Goh

HarperOne
An Imprint of HarperCollinsPublishers

HarperCollins books may be purchased for educational, business, or sales
promotional use. For information please e-mail the Special Markets Department
at SPsales@harpercollins.com.

HarperCollins website: http://www.harpercollins.com

FIRST HARPERCOLLINS PAPERBACK EDITION PUBLISHED IN 2017

Designed by Ralph Fowler
Artwork by Colin Goh. Used by permission.

Library of Congress Cataloging-in-Publication Data is available upon request.

ISBN 978–0–06–237887–3

22 23 24 25 26 LBC 13 12 11 10 9

There are many things in life
that suck. Joy isn't one of them.

To all who have taught me to access joy,
especially in my darkest hours, thank you.

Contents

How I Learned to Be Jolly for Fun and Profit

Let me tell you my story. Once upon a time, there was a smart and happy boy who, at twenty-one, had grown into a joyful, confident, and well-adjusted young man. That wasn't me.

I was born in Singapore in 1970. That year, tiny Singapore was a poor developing country with no natural resources. By the time I turned twenty-one, Singapore had become a rich country with one of the highest per-capita incomes in the world. It was the Singapore economic miracle. My family's fortune grew in tandem with that national economic miracle. My father had started his career as a ten-year-old hawker selling wares along the streets of downtown Singapore. A few years before I was born, he joined the army to get out of poverty. When I was an infant, we were so poor, my mother resorted to eating only one and a half meals a day to conserve what little money we had. Fast-forward twenty-one years: my father had retired from the army as a high-ranking officer and had gone on to become a wealthy business leader.

When I was twelve, I taught myself to program a computer, which back in 1982, was a big deal. By fifteen, I won my first of many national programming awards. Almost fifteen years after that, when I was twenty-nine, my programming skills landed me a job as one of the earliest engineers at a small startup company called Google (which has grown a little bigger since I joined in 2000). At Google, I was so notorious for my jolliness and humor that my job title became "Jolly Good Fellow (which nobody can deny)." It started as a joke, but it stuck after it made the front page of *The New York Times*.[1] I also did something at Google that should be quite out of character for an engineer: I led the creation of a mindfulness-based emotional intelligence course called Search Inside Yourself. It became the most popular course at Google and the subject of an international bestselling book of the same name, endorsed by the Dalai Lama and Jimmy Carter, former President of the United States. Almost overnight, I became widely recognized as an expert on topics that a geeky Asian engineer should have no business being associated with: emotional intelligence, mindfulness, compassion, and inner joy. I spoke at the White House about developing kindness and delivered a TED Talk at the United Nations about compassion.[2] *60 Minutes* interviewed me for a story on mindfulness,[3] and CNN did a story on my "algorithm for happiness."[4]

From this story, you would think that I have always been happy. Actually, nope. In fact, I spent most of my early life on the wrong end of the happiness spectrum. Up until I was twenty-one, I was miserable. Misery was my constant companion, and this constant companion smelled like it hadn't showered since Nixon was president.

Happiness was not something that came naturally to me—it was a skill I had to learn.

Happiness Is Highly Trainable

Once upon a time, a Chinese guy went to see a fortune-teller. After the fortune-teller read his palms carefully, she said to him, "You are miserable now, and you will continue to suffer misery until you turn forty." He asked excitedly, "What happens after forty? Will my misery finally go away?" And she said, "No, after forty, you'll get used to it." That was not me either.

Fortunately for me, my story had a much happier ending. I was miserable until I was twenty-one. That year, I learned that the ability to access joy is highly trainable. I developed the skills to access joy, and I became happy. This book is about those skills, so that you, too, can learn them and be happy.

Studies suggest that people have a remarkable ability to adapt to both good and bad fortune, and that we each have a relatively stable level of happiness that we eventually return to even after major positive or negative life events. A famous 1978 study, for example, shows that even people who won a lot of money in the lottery, or who were paralyzed in accidents, eventually returned to their average levels of happiness.[5] A 1996 study involving twins suggests that roughly half of our happiness is associated with our genetic makeup.[6] None of the other factors studied, including socioeconomic status, education, family income, marital status, or religiosity could account for more than 3 percent of the difference in people's happiness. In other words, you are born with a happiness set point that is mostly determined by your genes. A large part of our happiness depends on our luck in the genetic draw, and I just happened to draw a bad hand. I got a low happiness set point. I imagine a cartoon deity read my genetic chart as I was born and went, like, "Sorry, bro, sucks to be you. Bye."

Oh no! What to do? Fortunately, I found the solution. In the same way that physical qualities such as strength and agility are highly trainable, mental qualities such as joy and calmness are also highly trainable.

Pretend that you know nothing of the concept of physical fitness, and pretend that I just showed you how to do bicep curls by moving a dumbbell up and down with one arm, and then I tell you to do the same. You may reasonably think I'm stupid or something. The question you should ask me is, "Why? Why would I want to waste my time and energy moving a heavy object up and down?" (Among some engineers I know, this is known as WTF? For those of you who have to ask, WTF stands for "What is happening?!")

Once you understand the ideas behind exercise and physical fitness, bicep curls make perfect sense. Every time you move a dumbbell up and down, you strengthen your muscles a little bit more. If you do a lot of bicep curls and other weight-lifting exercises, you gain a physical quality known as strength. With strength, you can do things you could never imagine doing before. For example, you can now open really stubborn pickle jars and literally throw out the bad boyfriend. In addition to developing strength (and gaining the ability to literally throw out the bad boyfriend), though, you also develop something even more important: physical health and fitness. With physical health and fitness, every single aspect of your life improves. You have more energy, you suffer fewer sick days, and you become more successful at your work because you have more energy and fewer sick days. You look better in the mirror, you are confident, and you feel great. If you have never heard of the idea of physical training, the claim I just made should blow your mind, because I'm claiming that you can deliberately effect life-changing physiological changes with simple training exercises like repeatedly moving a heavy object up and down, and in doing so, improve every single aspect of your life.

In my long struggle with misery, quite by accident, I discovered the mental equivalent of physical exercise. I found that one can deliberately effect life-changing mental changes with simple training exercises—if you will, bicep curls for the mind. We can develop major mental skills like the ability to access joy on demand, and in doing so, improve every single aspect of our lives. The mental equivalent of physical exercise is meditation.

Meditation is another word for *mind training*. It is scientifically defined as "a family of mental training practices that are designed to familiarize the practitioner with specific types of mental processes."[7] To meditate, you just need to have a mind. To practice meditation is to practice with your mind, to get better at doing certain things with it, such as experiencing joy. Of particular interest to us is a form of meditation known as mindfulness meditation. It is one of many forms of meditation, in the same way jogging is one of many forms of exercise. Mindfulness is defined as "paying attention in a particular way: on purpose, in the present moment, and non-judgmentally."[8] So mindfulness is a specific way of paying attention, and mindfulness meditation means practicing this way of paying attention.

I started meditating because I was miserable enough to try anything. Back in those days in my part of Asia, meditation wasn't cool. In fact, it was the opposite of cool—it was kind of weird. We didn't have hippies in Singapore when I was growing up, but we did have our share of folks whom family members gossiped about with an odd mixture of fascination and embarrassment, and those were the type of people who tended to be associated with meditation. Worse still, there were no secular meditation teachers, so the only way to learn meditation back then was in Buddhist centers (which is why I came out of this experience determined to make meditation practices accessible in a secular form so people don't have to be Buddhists to benefit from them, but that's another story). Even worse still, in those days, Buddhism was perceived in some parts of Asia, including Singapore, as old, dusty, boring, and profoundly uncool. So a skinny, awkward, geeky young man trying hard to look cool to his friends had to be really desperate to try to learn meditation, and that was me.

Look at that Meng! -Tt!- Can you believe how uncool he looks?

Even back then, I had the vague sense that meditation was the solution to my misery, but I didn't know why or how. The breakthrough came in September of 1991, when I was a new undergraduate student at Nanyang Technological University, in Singapore. I attended a lecture on campus by a woman called Venerable Sangye Khadro. Sangye Khadro, also known as the author Kathleen McDonald, is an American woman who was ordained as a Tibetan Buddhist nun. The first thing I noticed about her was the calm and joyful dignity in the way she stood, walked, sat, and talked. I was immediately impressed. Then, right in the middle of her lecture, there was this one sentence, "It is all about cultivating the mind." When I heard that, in an instant, everything in my life suddenly made sense. Everything. I made two life-changing decisions right at that moment. First, I told myself, "From this moment

on, right here, right now, I am a Buddhist." Second, I decided to
learn to meditate, no matter how hard it would be.

Anyway, very soon after I decided to learn to meditate, I met my
first real meditation teacher. There is a popular saying in meditation
circles that "when the student is ready, the teacher appears." Either
that, or it was pure dumb luck. In any case, I met a revered meditation teacher from Sri Lanka called Godwin Samararatne who, in
my opinion, deserved every ounce of the tons of reverence people
heaped upon him. Despite his profound wisdom, he was able to
teach meditation in a way that even I could understand. He was the
first of many wise people from whom I have learned that happiness
is trainable, one joyful moment at a time.[9]

There is now no doubt in my mind whatsoever that meditation
can lead to happiness in real life. I know this because I am myself a
rather extreme example. My baseline happiness used to be misery,
which meant that when nothing was happening, I was miserable. It
meant that if something good happened, I would feel happier for a
while but then eventually return to misery. And it meant that despite
the prosperity and recognition and other kinds of worldly success
that came as I grew up, I wasn't happy. In a couple of years after I
started mind training, my baseline had shifted to jolly, which means
that when nothing was happening, I was jolly. When I experience
something painful, it's painful, but I eventually return to being jolly.

Wow.

People used to assume that baseline happiness is unchangeable,
but I am living proof that it can be moved from high negative to
high positive with only a few years of practice. I am certainly not
the only one. Even the masters of happiness needed training to get
to where they are. Take the Dalai Lama, for example, to whom joy
comes so readily that once, when asked by a reporter what was the
happiest moment of his life, he answered (with a mischievous glint

in his eyes), "Right now." Even the Dalai Lama was not always jolly, even he had to train his mind to be happy "right now," and even he has to practice every day.

Even the "happiest man in the world," the Tibetan Buddhist monk Matthieu Ricard, whose happiness has been famously measured and reported on since 2007,[10] would be the first to tell you he wasn't born happy. He has achieved lasting states of inner peace and joy (and what he modestly calls "some levels of inner freedom and compassion") thanks to a lifelong training inspired by his spiritual teachers. When I spoke to him about this, he emphasized that this is not a cliché about a small number of people being special. It is really about the training that he and his friends went through, which anybody can derive similar benefits from. Another person who has achieved extreme measures of happiness is Mingyur Rinpoche, in neuroscientist Richard Davidson's pioneering lab in Madison, Wisconsin. He openly admits that he suffered severe panic attacks as a child and that he overcame his panic attacks with his meditation practice.[11]

I think this is no accident—it is probably by design. We know this because even as far back as during the lifetime of the Buddha, around 500 BCE or so, an Indian king made the observation that Buddhist monks seemed remarkably peaceful and happy to him. More convincingly, to me, are the participants in my Search Inside Yourself class. The vast majority of those participants did little or no meditation before the class, but after just a few days or weeks of meditation, many of them reported meaningful increases in happiness. A 2003 study yields a similar finding, that just eight weeks of mindfulness training is enough to cause significant changes in the brain associated with increased happiness.[12]

These days, I'm in a good place—halfway?—on this continuum between Unhappy Average Joe or Miserable Average Jill at one end and His Holiness and other masters of happiness at the other. These days, I recently realized, I almost never lose my sense of humor anymore. Archbishop Desmond Tutu once said, "If you want to become an agent of change, you have to remember to keep your sense of humor." I agree: joy is an immensely powerful resource.

Okay, maybe I'm only a quarter of the way to immutable joy 24-7, but the more important point is that it's a continuum. That is, joy and happiness are highly trainable. Precisely: this is *why* they come so readily to His Holiness and other very happy people. They have been practicing their whole lives. This doesn't mean you have to be an octogenarian monk before you can be really happy, however, because long before you master happiness, all kinds of things start to get a whole lot better, as we will see.

Joy Independent of Sensual and Ego Pleasures

There was a man who had a skin condition that made his skin itch all the time. Every time he scratched his itch, he felt good. Then one day, a skillful doctor cured him of his skin condition, and he didn't have to scratch anymore. He realized that scratching his itch had felt good, but not having to scratch an itch at all feels even better.

We have a mind condition that makes us itch for two types of pleasure: pleasure of the senses and pleasure of the ego. When our senses are pleasantly stimulated, as when we eat something tasty, or our ego is pleasantly stimulated, as when we are praised for something we did, we feel joy, which is good. What is even better is if we can feel joy independent of sense or ego pleasure. For example, when we are eating chocolate, we experience joy, and when we are just sitting there not eating chocolate, we still experience joy. In order to do this, we train the mind to access joy even when it is free from stimulation. This is also the secret of raising your happiness set point.

To train the mind to access stimulus-free joy, we need to understand how joy arises independent of sensual stimulation and then cultivate those skills. They are three: easing, inclining, and uplifting.

1. Easing into Joy

The first skill we need in support of joy on demand is resting the mind to put it into a state of ease. When the mind is at ease, joy becomes more accessible, so part of the practice is learning to access that joy in ease, and then in turn, using the joy to reinforce the ease. I call this easing into joy: being joyful at rest, no ego stroking or sensual pleasure required. Cultivating this form of inner joy begins to free us from overreliance on sense and ego stimulation for pleasure. This means joy becomes increasingly available anyplace, anytime.

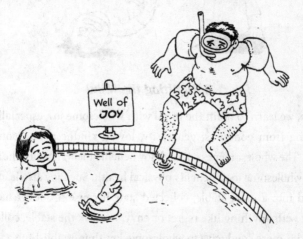

2. Inclining the Mind Toward Joy

Next, we learn to notice joy and give it our full attention. We learn where to look in order to see and appreciate joy that is already available to us, in moments that we hadn't noticed before. There is joy to be found in a calming breath and in the pleasures of ordinary activities. We invite this joy in. Inviting and noticing joy become part of our meditation practice as well as habits in everyday life. In time, with practice, the mind starts to get to know joy. It becomes familiar with joy like a close family member we can count on. The more the mind becomes familiar with joy, the more it perceives joy, inclines toward joy, and effortlessly creates the conditions conducive to joy.

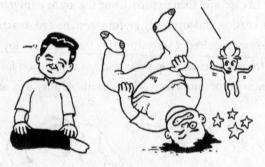

Maybe he's having trouble inclining because he's not very *lean*.

3. Uplifting the Mind

Here, we learn to uplift the mind with wholesome joy, especially joy arising from goodness, generosity, loving-kindness, and compassion. The wholesomeness of such joy benefits mental health the same way wholesome food benefits physical health. Such joy also leads the mind into a more stable, collected state because it doesn't have to fight with anything like regret or envy. In turn, the stable, collected mind is more conducive to wholesome joy, thus establishing a virtuous cycle.

With training in easing, inclining, and uplifting the mind comes the increasing ability to **access joy on demand** in most normal life circumstances (i.e., in the absence of overwhelming difficulties such as losing a livelihood or a loved one).

As an engineer, I thought you'd appreciate this hack of mine a little more...

After Google director Jonathan Berent learned these skills, he noticed a profound impact on his life. He told me, "I have found that I can at any moment take a conscious breath and access joy. In fact, this has been so helpful that I use my watch's chronometer to remind me to take at least one breath per hour when I am fully present to it. A couple years ago, I would have thought this was pointless. Joy on demand? You have to be kidding me. Now it is a reality to me, and I know it's possible at any moment."

Someone else I know experienced a change from doing one small practice in this book for a very short time. Janie had been unable to sleep well for many years. After practicing attending to the joy of loving-kindness (see Chapter 5) for two minutes, that night she slept better than she had in years. Now she practices loving-kindness daily and has been sleeping better since.

But wait, there's more. The same mental equipment we use to

train in uplifting our minds, inclining toward joy, and easing into joy gives us the strength and skills we need to deal with difficulties and emotional pain. I cannot promise that your life will be nothing but joyful in one breath or hours of training or by the time you reach the end of this book, but I can promise that whenever you can do these three things—easing, inclining, and uplifting—**what appears to be painful will be less painful, what is neutral will become joyful, and what is joyful will become even more joyful.**

(This is where you say, "Wow.")

If you have been unhappy, or you are happy and aspire to be even happier, know that your happiness set point can be upgraded. I know because I did it and I have seen many others do it in the mind training program I taught at Google. I have also seen scientific studies that have measured it. Of course, Buddhist monks and other contemplative people have been doing it for thousands of years, but it's not something in the water in the Himalayas—it's something you can do too, wherever you are.

You may well ask, if this kind of reliable and lasting joy is so accessible, why haven't more people found it? Why does it seem so elusive? I think the main problem is most people aren't aware that joy independent of sensual or ego stimulation is even possible. Or if we've heard of it, many of us think it is unattainable so we don't even try. We don't know it's something that every single one of us can learn. Some believe you need a lot of money to experience joy, while others believe you can only find happiness if you give up everything and live in a hut in the woods. You might think you need to meditate for many years to access joy, but as you will see in Chapter 2, you can begin to experience benefits in one breath.

If we think joy comes only from buying stuff, consuming stuff, becoming a sleazy tycoon, or running for president after becoming a sleazy tycoon, then joy will be elusive.

In modern society, with modern technology, pleasure is more accessible than ever, all around us, on demand. Our lack of joy is certainly not for lack of ways to gratify our egos and senses. However, the joy that comes from these sources is inherently problematic since it depends on external factors out of our control. (That YouTube selection seems completely within our control, until our Internet access stops working.)

By contrast, joy that comes from within—from a peaceful mind as a result of taking a few breaths, joy from being kind toward others (which involves other people but does not depend on them), joy from our own generosity, joy from doing the right thing—all this joy is ours to have, independent of circumstances. If we do accidentally lose our joy, or something really bad happens and overwhelms us, there's still joy in knowing we can get it back. We all have an infinite resource at our disposal, no matter how constrained or difficult our circumstances, and that resource is joy. Joy isn't elusive when you know where and how to look.

Joy Leads to Success

Life is weird. Sometimes you find something only when you stop looking for it. Once, for example, I needed a specific cable for my computer. I searched everywhere in the house and could not find it. After an hour, I gave up and told myself I'd buy another cable the next day, and a few minutes after I gave up, I saw it sitting on a shelf three feet in front of me.

I discovered I had a similar relationship with success. When I started to become skillful at accessing joy that is independent of sensual or ego pleasures, I became much happier, and my desperate desire for worldly success also began to wane. Since I could now be happy with or without being rich, and with or without "proving myself" to the world, I didn't see why I should be so obsessed with being "successful" anymore. I thought I was giving up on my shot at worldly success and I would end up as a cautionary tale for all Asian "tiger moms." The opposite happened and I became even more successful.

I later found out why: joy leads to happiness, and happiness leads to success. But first, what is the difference between joy and happiness? I like to let Matthieu Ricard define happiness. I figure "the happiest man in the world" ought to know. As Matthieu points out, happiness is "a deep sense of flourishing that arises from an exceptionally healthy mind . . . not a mere pleasurable feeling, a fleeting emotion, or a mood, but an optimal state of being."[13] Joy, in contrast, *is* a pleasurable feeling. It is an emotion. It is in the moment, while happiness is more of a net effect, over time, of mental health and fitness and personal flourishing. Joy is a building block of happiness. A happy life is made up of many moments of joy. While happiness doesn't mean every moment is pure joy, there is no such thing as a joyless path to happiness. The ability to access joy on demand enabled me to build a happy life. In this sense, joy leads to happiness.

What about happiness and success? It turns out I had it all wrong. My Asian upbringing had led me to believe that success leads to happiness, that one day, when I am successful, I will be happy. In fact, the opposite is true. Success does not lead to happiness; instead, happiness leads to success. This relationship between success and happiness has been extensively studied. My friend Shawn Achor brilliantly calls it the "The Happiness Advantage," which is also the title of his bestselling book.[14] Citing hundreds of studies carried out over decades, Shawn makes a convincing case that happiness is a major advantage in the pursuit of success. As he summed it up in a 2011 *Harvard Business Review* article, "The single greatest advantage in the modern economy is a happy and engaged workforce."[15] Happiness raises sales by 37 percent, productivity by 31 percent, and accuracy on tasks by 19 percent. Happiness also makes people more popular and better at their jobs, or better in school if they are in school. It makes people healthier, too, and better off by myriad other quality-of-life metrics. Happiness even increases creativity, as we will see in Chapter 1. This would not be such good news if happiness were out of our control and simply a matter of luck. It is great news because joy and happiness are trainable, and that's what *Joy on Demand* is about.

If you want to be successful, I highly recommend learning to be happy first. It is possible to become successful without first learning to be happy, but I strongly recommend against it, because if you are unhappy before you are successful, you are likely to be even more unhappy after. For example, based on my own experience becoming financially successful and that of other wealthy people I know, I have found wealth to be a personality multiplier. If you are cruel and unkind, then being wealthy will make you even more cruel and unkind, because you don't even have survival-related reasons to be nice to anyone anymore. If, instead, you are kind and generous, then being wealthy will make you more so, because wealth provides more opportunities for doing so.

Since wealth is a personality multiplier, it is also an experience multiplier. If you are miserable when you are middle class, you will likely be even more miserable when you are wealthy, because all the mental states that cause you to be miserable, such as greed, cruelty, paranoia, and inner turmoil, get multiplied. Similarly, if you're happy when you're middle class, you're likely to be even happier wealthy, for the same reason; mental states that brought you happiness—such as generosity, kindness, and inner peace—multiply, thereby multiplying happiness.

So it is always good to learn to be happy, and it is especially useful to do it *before* becoming successful. Then, it will help you become successful, and it will help you enjoy success.

A Virtuous Cycle

Some motivation for this book arose from the response of readers of my first book, *Search Inside Yourself,* that while they appreciated the many wondrous benefits of training in mindfulness, it seemed like a lot of work. It was daunting to think that they couldn't enjoy its benefits (hint: joy) without meditating for an hour a day. This really isn't necessary. Very simple, efficient changes in perspective and easy practices that anyone can do have the power to effect dramatic change and enormous benefit.

Fortunately, being a lazy meditator myself, I know how to make meditation easier than even the simple practices I wrote about in *Search Inside Yourself,* and the key is joyful practice.

Confucius once said, "Never buy just one when you can buy two for the same price." I'm just kidding—Confucius didn't actually say that, but he *could* have, being wise and all.

There are some really nice things in life that naturally reinforce each other, and in doing so, they form virtuous cycles with each other. For example, if you enjoy performing an activity that requires some level of skill (such as juggling, surfing, or playing a musical instrument), you may find yourself doing it a lot and getting better at it. And as you get better at it, you may derive even more enjoyment from it. And when you enjoy it more, you do it even more and get even better at it, and so on. So in this case, skillfulness and enjoyment form a virtuous cycle in which one strengthens the other—hence you end up benefiting from both at once, at no extra cost, thus winning the approval of the fictitious Confucius I made up.

Joy and meditation are another pair of really nice things that form a virtuous cycle with each other. Meditation is training of the mind. Joy becomes highly accessible in a trained mind. With training, the mind learns to access inner joy with increasing ease and frequency. At the same time, the joyful mind is at peace, a peaceful mind is easily focused, and a focused mind becomes more trainable, thereby making meditation practice even more effective. Thus a virtuous and joyful cycle forms. Once you put it into motion, the meditation practice that perhaps you thought you'd never have can be sustained, and joy becomes a dominant factor in daily life.

In this book, we will explore this relationship and ways to initiate the turning of this powerful, joyful, virtuous cycle. It is through this cycle that we eventually arrive where the masters of happiness are, where every moment is the happiest of our lives because we always have joy on demand.

The Wondrous Benefits, In Case You Haven't Heard

It goes without saying that one benefit of joy on demand is: joy. Duh. More and more, as you practice, your days will fill up with moments and even extended periods of joy. Not every moment will be joyful, but knowing that you can count on joy to happen again, and in increasing amounts, tends to improve your overall mood.

Inner joy relies on inner peace, so that is our practical starting point: Chapters 2 and 3 show you how to ease into joy. You will learn to calm the mind and find some peace in the midst of this crazy, speedy world where joy can happen.

In the next chapter, we incline toward joy. If you are reading this book because you feel like a stranger to joy, I invite you to Chapter 4, where you will be (re)introduced to the joy in you and the joy in the world. This chapter helps you get acquainted with your inner joy. With practice, you can become so inclined toward and ultimately familiar with joy that it becomes a habit.

Compassion and kindness arise from inner peace and joy. Compassion is both the fruition and the multiplier of joy—another one of those cycles of goodness. In other words: joy makes you a kinder, more compassionate person, and kindness and compassion bring you more joy! Chapter 5 describes this cycle in more detail, with exercises that will help you keep it going. This is the uplifting part.

With inner peace, inner joy, and compassion, you get the whole enchilada: confidence and charisma, creativity and innovation, self-awareness, well-being and emotional resilience, happiness, humor, popularity, courage, and success in every arena, plus personal freedom and world peace. Joy is the wellspring of all good things, even luck. We will relish these benefits in more detail in Chapters 1 and 7.

Chapter 6 is about dealing with pain. I wish you all the joy in the world, my friends, but the fact is that sometimes terrible things happen. Sometimes we have really shitty days (or months). Always there is suffering in the world. Sometimes the odds of circumstance stack up so high against joy that all we can do is to hunker down and bear witness. This chapter explains how to apply the skills you have already been practicing (from the previous chapters) when you are facing emotional pain. It also reveals pain's best-kept secret, which may surprise you (spoiler alert): joy and pain can coexist. Just because you are in pain doesn't mean you can't also access joy. Don't worry, you will get better at this with practice. And this is the silver lining of pain: whatever else it is, it's an opportunity to practice getting better at working with pain. Remember, with practice, what is joyful will be even more joyful, what is neutral will be joyful, and what appears to be painful will be less painful.

My friends, we are very lucky. We have an unprecedented opportunity. We live in an age when things that we didn't think we could study scientifically—happiness, kindness, mindfulness, peace, and so on—now we can, because we have the technology to measure them. Over thousands of years, human suffering hasn't qualitatively changed. What has changed is the meeting of science and ancient wisdom, making powerful practices that give us access to joy on demand widely understandable, and because they are widely understandable, they can become widely accessible.

I wrote this book to help make joy on demand more understandable and more accessible to you. I hope you will enjoy it.

CHAPTER ONE

Joy Becomes You

*Surprising (and Not-So-Surprising)
Benefits of Mind Training*

Confucius said, "If you cannot choose between one of many good options, just choose them all." No, Confucius didn't say that either—I made it up, but once again, he could have said it because he is so wise and all. It is a common misperception that certain good things are mutually exclusive. For example, you might think that in order to be successful, you cannot be compassionate, because everybody on Wall Street knows that compassion is for chumps. Or some people believe calm and charisma don't go together. They assume charisma depends on wild enthusiasm and manic smiles, and being calm is boring. In fact, as we will see in this chapter, compassion and success, calm and charisma, and many other good things in life from creativity to resilience, are mutually reinforcing.

And they all come from joy. Or if not directly from joy, they turn out to be side effects of the training that enables us to access joy. For when you learn to access joy on demand (see: this book) the effects go far beyond isolated moments of joy. Joy can improve every aspect of life. It resets happiness set points, turning miserable people into jolly ones. With practice, joy can become your personality and your whole life. As if that wasn't enough, it also makes you more attractive. Joy becomes you, in every sense of becoming. Joy is very much a package deal. Confucius would approve. Welcome to the whole enchilada, with extra sauce and a free toy.

Even the Basic Benefits of Mind Training Are Life Changing

Reliable access to joy begins with mind training. In the beginning, meditation was very difficult for me. (Remember, meditation is mind training. When I am referring to specific meditation practices like sitting meditation, I will say so.) It didn't seem to have anything to do with joy. Happily, once I figured out how to do it, it wasn't long—a few short months—before it started to change my life. And now I see mind training has everything to do with joy. With this book, you get the benefit of my experience of learning the hard way so you can expect things to get better for you in even less time, and with less difficulty and more joy, than I had. You're welcome.

The first, most basic and possibly most important benefit of mind training is **the ability to calm the mind on demand.** Eventually, with practice, you will find yourself able to abide in a calm mind during most sitting meditations. Better still, you will also find yourself increasingly able to apply this skill in "real life" outside of sitting meditation. This one skill alone may be life changing. For example, one student in my class, after just a few weeks of training, found himself able to refrain from saying something nasty to his mother-in-law. That changed *his* life, no doubt.

Of course, now the challenge is to get my mother-in-law to take up meditation too.

It's never easy to get one's mum-in-law to stay mum.

The ability to calm the mind on demand also has profound implications for leadership. Imagine you're in a meeting room with your coworkers in the middle of a crisis. Everybody is frazzled, but you alone can calm down and think, because you alone have developed the skill to calm the mind on demand. What happens? Everybody in the room is going to look at you and say to himself or herself, "Wow, this person is a leader." And they would be right, because that is leadership. A key part of leadership is precisely the ability to think calmly and clearly under fire. Hence, by training yourself in calming the mind, you become a more effective leader.

The second basic benefit of mind training is **clarity of mind.** With calmness of mind comes clarity. Actually, no, for many beginners, with calmness of mind comes sleepiness, but once you develop the ability to remain calm without necessarily being sleepy, then you get to abide in a delicious state of mind that is calm and clear at the same time. It is like a pot of sediment-filled water left undisturbed for a while—when the water is calm over a period of time, the sediment settles to the bottom and the water becomes clear. Similarly, when the mind is calm over a period of time, some of the noisy mental activity quiets down and the mind becomes clear.

The obvious effect of this clarity is increased self-awareness. As the mind clears, so does our perception into the process of emotion, the process of cognition, and the process of self. This strengthens at least two aspects of self-awareness: emotional awareness, where the subtleties of our moment-to-moment experience of emotion become increasingly discernible; and self-assessment, where we consider our own identity, inclinations, resources, and weaknesses with more objectivity.

The third basic benefit of mind training is **emotional resilience,** especially in response to emotional pain. As we will see in Chapter 6, emotional resilience works in three steps: attentional, affective, and cognitive. When hit by an episode of emotional pain, first we apply an attentional strategy, temporarily redirecting attention to the breath and the body, and by doing that, calming the mind. By itself, calming the mind solves half the problem on the spot, but that's only the first step. In the second step, the affective step, we manage the emotionality involved. Here, we mindfully and objectively perceive the emotions as they happen in the body. After a while, we may recognize that even these afflictive emotions are merely sensations in the body and that they are constantly changing, arising and ceasing over time. We then manage the feelings by treating them with kind friendliness if possible, or if not possible, at least sitting with them in equanimity. At this point, we arrive at some degree of composure. With the third, cognitive step, we gain a broader, wiser, and more compassionate perspective. With a composed mind, we are able to see things in a different light. For example, we take this opportunity to understand ourselves and to grow. If the emotional pain arises from a situation involving other people, we can take this opportunity to understand them and their suffering. If the emotional pain arises from failure, we can figure out how to use it as building blocks for future success, remembering that the Chinese word for *crisis* suggests both danger and opportunity. In other words, we apply the cognitive step to increasing our wisdom and compassion, and in doing so, reducing the causes of our own future suffering.

Mind training enables emotional resilience. In mind training, we practice calming the mind in difficult situations, perceiving the process of emotion at high resolution, and cultivating compassion and objectivity, thereby strengthening our ability to take all three steps when we're faced with emotional pain.

Any one of the three basic benefits of mind training—mental calm, mental clarity, and emotional resilience—is, by itself, life changing, and with practice all meditators can acquire all three. Without a doubt, meditation changed my life (for the better, in case you need to ask). With increasing calmness, clarity, and resilience, I became increasingly capable of overcoming the suffering in my life. Meditation turned out to be the solution to my misery. Honestly, that doesn't suck. And I know it isn't just me. For example, looking back on the time when she ran a startup called Locket, founder and CEO Yunha Kim describes how the basic benefits of mind training have made a difference for her:

I was under a lot of pressure. The more money we raised, the more pressure I felt—not just for my company's success but also for my performance as a young, first-time entrepreneur and leader. Later, we had to pivot our product and lay off half of the team, many of which I worked and lived with. I can't really describe how stressed and miserable I was during that time. I wasn't sleeping or eating enough, and the uncertainty of the company's future really consumed me. Yet, I had to put on my happy and confident CEO face for others.

I decided to see a therapist, who introduced me to mindfulness and meditation. I was skeptical at first, because I thought it was something only hippies and monks do. I was raised as a Christian, and I hesitated to try anything associated with other religions. But after trying meditation a few times, I was surprised to find clarity, both in my heart and in my mind. So I began to meditate every morning for ten minutes. It's been a couple years now since I started, and it's made a difference in my life. At first, I enjoyed the clarity it brought to my thoughts. But over time, I came to appreciate the calmness of mind.

There are times when I am restless and cranky but without an obvious reason. I feel it in my body—my breath is shorter and shallower, my hands and feet fidget. Meditation helps me identify the source. For instance, I once discovered my restlessness at work resulted from an unresolved argument with my mother the night before. In another instance, I was anxious at a dinner with friends but observed that I was restless over a promised e-mail I was expecting from a colleague. It's been fascinating to me how my mind snowballs a small argument or a missed e-mail into something ominously bigger. Meditation hasn't solved everything for me, but the daily practice has often helped me simplify my life by untangling some of my mind's complexity, both big and small.[1]

But wait, there is more still. Beyond calmness, clarity, and resilience, there are other compelling benefits that I was not expecting when I started.

Creativity: It's Not a Bug—It's a Feature!

The calm and clear mind is alert and relaxed, especially when suffused with inner joy. And I have found the alert and relaxed mind to be highly conducive to **creativity.**

I initially made this discovery in an annoying sort of way: a lot of good ideas and insights came to me while I was meditating. If I had a problem I couldn't solve, or I got invited to give a speech where I didn't have the slightest idea what to talk about, the answers would come to me while I was meditating. At first, I found it really irritating. Here I was, trying my best to focus attention gently on my breath, and then a great idea would arise, and I would get all excited, but my formal meditation would effectively be over. It always used to end with me scolding myself, "Oh, great job. Now see what you've screwed up *this* time." Over time, though, I learned to accept this as a natural process of the mind and to take advantage of it. The mind that is alert and relaxed sometimes gets creative, and when that happens, I'll invite it to calm down so I can get back to my object of meditation, but if it doesn't, I'll just allow the creativity to run its full course while I observe the experience with equanimity. I'll come out of it with some new ideas and some practice of equanimity in the midst of excitement.

Or as a good software engineer would say, "That's not a bug—that's a feature!"

In fact, both the idea for writing this book and the entire framework of the book arose in my mind during meditation. Months had passed after I promised a second book to my agent, Stephanie, and still there was no book proposal. In fact, there was not a single word from me (no pun intended). When Stephanie started calling me about it, I told her that I was still waiting for the book to write itself. I said there were two things I knew about this book: First, it had to write itself. And second, when the book was ready to write itself, I would know. That assurance did not improve the quality or quantity of Stephanie's sleep—I don't know why.

Then, one day, during my daily meditation, my mind went into a state of deep calmness, and suddenly, out of nowhere, two thoughts arose. The first thought was, "The book is now ready to be written." The second thought, which arose immediately after the first but took the next two or three minutes to fully form, was the entire framework of this book. Ta-da!

When I realized how conducive the alert and relaxed mind was to creativity, the first question I asked myself was, "Is it just me?"

Maybe I was the only person who became creative during meditation, maybe because I'm weird or something. I certainly haven't
seen a Zen master jumping up in the middle of sitting meditation
and wildly shouting, "Eureka! Eureka!" But over time, the evidence
I've seen convinced me that this effect is highly replicable. The first
pieces of evidence came from some of the students in my own class,
the early participants of the Search Inside Yourself course at Google. Several students reported becoming more creative at solving
problems, especially during or immediately after their sitting meditation. One engineer even told me that the solutions to the two most
difficult engineering problems he had to solve both came to him
during mindfulness practice, and because of that, he got promoted.

How does this work? From a first-person perspective, I can describe it with a pebble analogy. If you come to a lake where the wind
is strong and the water is choppy, and then if you drop a pebble into
that lake, it will cause a ripple, but because the water is choppy, you
can't see the ripple clearly. Drop a pebble into a calm lake, however,
and it makes a beautiful, circular ripple that you can clearly see.
Creativity seems to happen when random ideas arise and the mind
perceives them clearly and, more important, captures the novel, remote, or unexpected associations between these ideas. If the mind is
cluttered, noisy, or agitated, it is like dropping pebbles into turbulent
water—you don't see a lot of nice ripples, and you can't see how the
ripples form patterns with each other. However, when the mind is
alert and relaxed at the same time, relaxation gives random ideas
space to arise and play, and alertness lets us see them and their connections, just like dropping pebbles into a placid lake.

Beyond my own first-person experience, I later learned that the
relationship between relaxed attention and creativity is well-known
among people who rely on creativity for a living. Steve Jobs, for example, famously said:

If you just sit and observe, you will see how restless your mind is. If you try to calm it, it only makes it worse, but over time it does calm, and when it does, there's room to hear more subtle things—that's when your intuition starts to blossom and you start to see things more clearly and be in the present more. Your mind just slows down, and you see a tremendous expanse in the moment. You see so much more than you could see before. It's a discipline; you have to practice it.[2]

Another example comes from David Kelley and Tom Kelley, who strongly advocate what they call "relaxed attention" as a foundation of creativity. I would think the Kelleys know something about the topic. David and Tom are, respectively, founder and partner of IDEO, the global design company renowned internationally for creativity and innovation.

This topic has also been studied scientifically. For example, the work of neuroscientists like John Kounios, Mark Jung-Beeman, Joydeep Bhattacharya, and others established a link between the aha moment and alpha brainwaves. Creative insights often come along with alpha waves, especially in the right hemisphere of the brain. Alpha waves are related to nonarousal. They are often associated with relaxing activities such as strolling, taking a warm shower, and yes, meditation.

In practice, creative types already know instinctively that an alert and relaxed mind is highly conducive to creativity, and they know how to activate that state of mind. That is why they know to go for walks, play games, or take a warm shower if they get stuck while solving a problem. However, my own experience and that of some others strongly suggest that if you also add meditation to your repertoire, you can have even more creative breakthroughs as you learn to reach higher levels of both alertness and relaxation, and you can do so on demand. Neuroscientist John Kounios talks about an expert Zen meditator who took part in one of the CRA (Compound Remote Associate) insight experiments. For these experiments, participants have thirty seconds to think of a word that can be combined with each of three other words, for example *sauce, crab,* and *pine* (answer: *apple*). In the meditator's case, at first, his ability to focus worked against him, and he couldn't solve any of the puzzles. Then he figured out how to use his extraordinary powers of cognitive control to *un*-focus, to let go and let his brain make what Kounios believes were the necessary associations in the right hemisphere of the brain for the solution to occur. After that, he was unstoppable, solving all the puzzles the experimenters gave him.[3]

Not only is the alert and relaxed mind highly conducive to creativity, but studies have shown that a joyful mind is also highly conducive to creativity.[4] One study even shows that a joyful mind's influence on creativity lasts up to two days after the positive mood was felt.[5] In other words, if you are happy today, you are more creative today, tomorrow, and the day after, regardless of how you feel tomorrow and the day after! Why are joy and relaxation both so conducive to creativity? I think it is because, as we will see in the next chapter, a joyful mind is a relaxed mind (also vice versa); therefore, similar mental factors are probably at play.

I was surprised that my meditation practice was conducive to creativity. To me, however, the most surprising benefit of mind training came next.

Surprisingly Confident

One of the biggest surprise discoveries of my life is that self-confidence can be trained by putting my butt onto a meditation cushion.

When I was younger, I was cocky. I mistook my cockiness for confidence, but they turned out to be vastly different creatures. The biggest difference is that cockiness, unlike confidence, is necessarily fueled by conceit. Another big difference is fragility. Cockiness is very fragile. When some external conditions feed my conceit, cockiness flies to dizzying heights, and then when I experience some failure, the cockiness immediately breaks in midair and crashes to the ground with pain directly proportional to the altitude of the previous height. Confidence, however, is highly sustainable because it is independent of success or failure. Cockiness is also inauthentic. When I feel cocky, there is always a facade I have to put up to show the world how wonderful I supposedly am, while deep inside, I suffer agonizing insecurity anticipating the next crash. Confidence, in contrast, has its basis on seeing things as they are, so by its very nature, it is quite incompatible with inauthenticity.

Can meditation really make me less cocky?

After a few years of practicing meditation, I began to discover a feeling of confidence growing inside of me that, I realized later, is different from cockiness. Over the years, this confidence has successfully weathered both the giddy disorientation of success and adulation, and the soul-crushing pain of failure and dishonor. For me, discovering that meditation can lead to confidence was very surprising. The idea that somebody as flawed as me is capable of, over time, shifting some distance from cockiness to confidence is even more surprising.

Upon reflection, I realized that this confidence has three wholesome sources:

1. Confidence arising from knowing

2. Confidence arising from equanimity

3. Confidence arising from resilience

1. Confidence Arising from Knowing

Knowledge is confidence. There are three aspects of confidence that arise from knowing. The first aspect, which has very little to do with meditation, is **knowing your stuff.** If you walk into a room to talk about a specific topic and you are familiar with the materials, or better still, you're an expert, or even better, you are one of the world's top experts, then you walk into that room with confidence. That goes without saying.

There is, however, another aspect of confidence that arises from knowing that is even more powerful than the first, and that is **knowing yourself.** Knowing yourself means strong self-awareness, both at the level of emotional awareness (discerning your emotions in your body from one moment to the next) and self-assessment (knowing your abilities, limitations, resources, and habits). With enough self-awareness, you know how to play to your strengths, you know how to compensate for your weaknesses, you can navigate skillfully in most situations, and there's no skeleton in your closet that you don't already know about, so there's nothing about you that's going to

shock you. Occasionally you discover things about yourself that surprise you, but by and large, they are not surprising enough to floor
you. Because of that, you are comfortable in your own skin. When
you are comfortable in your own skin, it shows. Wherever you go,
there's a certain quiet confidence that just presents itself.

What does this come from? It comes mostly from mindfulness. When you practice mindfulness of body and mindfulness of
emotions, over time, you develop a strong self-awareness, and this
self-awareness leads to the type of self-confidence that comes from
knowing yourself.

What if there is something you need to know but don't know—
where is the confidence in that? There is an additional aspect of confidence that arises from knowing: **knowing that you can know.** In
other words, whatever you need to know, you are fully capable of
learning. The person who best illustrates this aspect of confidence
to me is one of my main meditation teachers, meditation master
Shinzen Young.

When Shinzen was becoming accomplished as a meditation
teacher, he developed a conviction, which I totally agree with, that
if meditation (which he calls "the internal science and technology
of the East") were to successfully mate and cross-fertilize with the
science and technology of the West, it will change the world dramat-
ically, for the better. So he set out to gain expertise in science in order
to become an active participant of intelligent dialogue between the
meditation world and the scientific world. There was only one problem: he was terrible at math and science in school. That was one of
his biggest pain points in his youth—it scarred him emotionally for
many years thereafter—and now, as a matured adult, it had become
the biggest barrier to what he felt was one of his most important
tasks. What to do? What to do?

Shinzen pondered on it and realized he was now a different person from the kid who did dreadfully at school. He was still terrible in math and science, but he had one important skill he hadn't had when he was a kid: he now had some mastery over his mind. He conjectured that with his mastery of mind, he could learn anything, anything, even (gulp!) math, and once he aced the math, he could ace the science. So he started teaching himself math and science, starting with multiplication tables and fifth-grade math, and then eventually working his way up to graduate-level math and science. Today, he is an admired pioneer at the intersection between meditation and science.

How did Shinzen do it? He said three things helped. First, he now had great power of concentration. In the past, after the second or third time he read something in a math textbook he couldn't understand, he would just give up. Now, he would just keep coming back with the same intense concentration until he got it. Second, he was able to manage the negative self-talk. He had a conviction that he could not do math, he had frequent and strongly negative emotional reactions against learning math, and the incessant self-talk that kept saying, "Who are you kidding? You'll never be able to do this shit!" (Yes, even widely admired meditation masters use the s-word). He dealt with them by breaking them up into manageable chunks and then using techniques similar to the attentional, affective, and cognitive strategies you'll find in Chapter 6 for dealing with painful emotions. The third thing he did was apply his power of empathy to gaining insights into mathematicians as people and then internalizing a "math geek" into his own personality. Feeling like he was someone who could do math, identifying as a math geek from the inside out, he wasn't intimidated by math anymore. In time, he went from somebody who had to relearn even multiplication tables to someone with expertise in graduate-level math. Math went from a long-running source of emotional pain to a huge source of joy for him.[6]

The lesson from Shinzen: With meditation, you gain some mastery of mind, and once you have that, you can gain expertise in any subject. That assurance that you can learn anything creates confidence.

2. Confidence Arising from Equanimity

The second source of confidence is confidence arising from equanimity. This comes in part from **the ability to calm the mind on demand.** As mentioned, the ability to calm the mind is one of the basic benefits of meditation. With sufficient practice, it becomes a skill: you can calm the mind on demand some meaningful percentage of the time, no matter how bad things get. If you know you can do that, you can walk into any room with some degree of confidence.

When you hear people dispensing advice like this, you wonder if they actually practice what they preach. In my case, quite unfortunately, I get to practice this a lot because my work requires me to be in the public spotlight more than I like to be. (It is no accident that the next three examples all take place in public speaking situations.) Being in the public eye is always nerve-racking because when you screw something up, it's very public. On one particular day, I was given the wonderful opportunity to screw up on TV. I was on CNBC, being interviewed on the floor of the New York Stock Exchange. It was a live interview being broadcast nationally and worldwide. And then, I forgot my lines. I was planning to talk about the three ways to settle the mind (see Chapter 3). When I got to item number two, I forgot what item number two was. "The second way to do it is . . . (blank)." I had my Rick

Perry oops moment. On live TV, broadcast worldwide. Oh no! What to do? What to do?

I could feel panic arising in my body. Then my training kicked in and I was able to calm the panic down before it showed. I stayed composed. It took me five seconds to recover, which when you're on live TV, is a very long time. But I remained so calm that when I later saw the recording, it didn't look like a disaster. It appeared like I was "deliberating" on what I was going to say. None of my friends who saw it knew that anything was gravely amiss. So now you know my secret. The next time I look like I'm deliberating, maybe I'm just gently panicking inside.

Another aspect of confidence arising from equanimity is **the ability to hold your ego very lightly.** I describe this as the willingness for your ego to be as big as a mountain and as small as a grain of sand at the same time. Once again, being an occasional public figure gives me plenty of uncomfortable opportunities to practice this. It happens, for example, when I get invited to speak to an audience that I believe is far more qualified than I am. Once, I was invited to speak in an Asian country to an auditorium full of the top Buddhist leaders in that country on the topic of Buddhism in the modern world. There were many senior, serious-looking monastics, heads of major temples, leaders of lay Buddhist organizations, and leading academics. And who was I? As far as I was concerned, I was just some engineer from California.

Here again, I was able to apply my training. I looked at the audience and felt tiny because each person in the audience knew ten times more Buddhism than I did with one hand tied behind their back. However, I also felt tiny in a wholesome way: I was there entirely to serve this group of people, so my own ego and needs were totally irrelevant. At the same time, in order serve in a way that this audience deserved, I needed to believe that I deserved to be standing in front of them, speaking to them as if I knew something that they didn't. And, in fact, I did. I may not have one-tenth their Buddhist scholarship or practice, but it is possible that I may be among the top experts in the world in the application of wisdom practices in the modern setting, and because of that, I likely have some hard-earned insights to share that even the top scholars may find valuable. There had to be a voice in my head willing to say those words to myself: "I am a master of this subject matter. I deserve to be here." (And a second voice arises in reaction that says, "Me?" And the original voice replies, "Yes, you, and get used to it, <expletive used to refer to oneself>.") Based on that, I allowed my ego to be (almost embarrassingly) big enough to fill the whole room. Hence, I allowed my ego to simultaneously be tiny and humongous at the same time. The trick was to focus on two attitudes: service and humor. Focusing on serving the people in front of me, I allowed my ego to be any size it needed to be in order to serve, and I maintained my humor at the absurdity of the situation.

Near the end of the session, a stern-looking monk sitting in the front row (presumably very senior, as he got to sit front and center with a nameplate at his seat in a language I don't read) asked me a question, which, I imagine, one can interpret as a loaded question. He asked, through simultaneous translation, "Of the four levels of enlightenment as defined in traditional Buddhism, which level are you at?" I noticed some tension in the room as he spoke. I looked at him intently, flashed my usual naughty smile, made a circular shape with the fingers of my right hand, and clearly pronounced, "Ze-ro." And then I laughed. That monk started laughing, the translator was laughing into my earpiece, and everybody in the auditorium was laughing. After the laughter died down, I further explained, "Seriously, you are the true Buddhist masters, and I'm just an engineer.

What do I know? I just hope that whatever little bit I know was useful to you." The monk nodded slightly with a smile.

I think that talk went well. How did I know? When Buddhist nuns clamor around you for selfies after you speak, you probably did something right.

In retrospect, I realized that I had handled that monk's question in the most skillful way I could without even thinking. I could have been defensive, offended, angry, or insecure, and I could have acted in a very unskillful way. I learned that if I just focus on service and humor, then I will most likely not screw it up.

The ability to calm the mind comes from the focused-attention aspect of meditation training. The ability to hold your ego very lightly comes partly from mindfulness training and the self-awareness that comes from mindfulness. It also comes from the sustainable joy that arises from a calm mind and the sense of service that comes from compassion training (see Chapter 5). And, yes, if you practice mindfulness of your own eventual death at least once a day (see Chapter 4), your ego becomes quite malleable.

3. Confidence Arising from Resilience

What happens on days when knowledge fails and equanimity also fails? That brings us to the third source of confidence, confidence arising from resilience. One aspect of confidence arising from resilience is the **ability to recover:** knowing that when things fail, I can always eventually recover. I know my practice is sufficiently strong that if somebody says something to me where I feel embarrassed, offended, or triggered, I know that even if I lose my cool, I can recover it in five to ten seconds under most circumstances. That gives me confidence walking into a room. In the somewhat longer run, I know that if I suffer some sort of very unpleasant setback—say I'm publicly insulted by somebody I thought was an ally or I find out I didn't get the promotion I thought I deserved—I know I can recover in four to five hours in most situations, twenty-four hours at most. That gives me confidence doing my day-to-day work. And ultimately, I have faith that no matter how bad things become, if I lose everything, if I become crippled in a car accident, I know that I will probably go through some period of severe depression, but I also know that at my current level of practice, I can recover my sanity and composure in no more than six to twelve months. That gives me confidence living this life.

I have an almost-funny example of practicing recovery in a short timescale. On that particular day, I was giving a TED Talk hosted at the United Nations. It was the most nervous I've ever been about public speaking. I knew that TED Talks get watched a lot, so I knew that eventually some ridiculously high number of people (perhaps approaching one million) would see it, especially since it was hosted at the United Nations. I arrived in New York early just so I could spend an entire day practicing my fourteen-minute speech in my hotel room, in front of a mirror, dressed in my Chinese suit (literally a full dress rehearsal). It turned out, even that preparation was not enough for me.

While I was delivering my TED Talk on stage, halfway into my talk, I got so nervous my right leg started shaking. At least I had the clarity of mind to tell myself, "If you don't fix this problem soon, history is going to remember you as the guy who fell off the stage at TED." With my meditation training, I was at least able to calm my mind enough to continue speaking as if nothing was wrong, but the shaking didn't stop. So I subtly shifted my weight to my left leg and continued speaking. After a short while, the right leg stopped shaking, but the left leg started shaking, so I subtly shifted my weight back and continued talking.

MINDFUL RIVERDANCING WITH MENG!

After a few minutes, I recovered. I'm happy to report that I did not fall off the stage at TED, hence the annals of history contain one fewer comedic story at my expense. When I later got to watch the video on ted.com, I was astonished to see the guy onstage confident and showing no signs of nervousness. And I was there—that guy was me! I know precisely the anxiety he felt inside, but at the same time, he was very composed, even while holding that anxiety, confident that he could recover. That was when I realized that twenty years of meditation practice was not a complete waste of my time.

Another aspect of confidence arising from resilience is more powerful than all the other aspects of confidence we have talked about, possibly powerful enough that even if you master only this one aspect alone, you can live your entire life with impeccable confidence. This is **the willingness to bear witness to our own pain and failure.** To be willing and able to clearly see this self—this wretched, useless self—to see all his pain, to see all his failings, his desperate clinging on to all things pleasant and his frenzied aversion to all things unpleasant, to see all the suffering involved in having this human form manifest in him, to be willing and able to bear witness to all of that with composure and kindness—that is an immense source of confidence. Better still, if you can witness all that pain and failure within yourself and have the composure and kindness be sufficiently strong for a gentle joy to arise and permeate even in the midst of witnessing all that pain and failure, then you will have no more fear, and you will embody the confidence of fearlessness. This is one of the highest levels of confidence you can have.

Some years ago, while I was struggling with an extended episode of severe emotional distress, I made the stupid decision of scheduling a ten-day formal meditation retreat right in the middle of it. In general, meditation retreats are tough for most people. Your back hurts from sitting for hours a day, you battle sleepiness (and guilt) while you're sitting, but you don't sleep well at night when you're supposed to, you can't talk, the communal toilet is either too close to your room or too far away, and you're away from all things comforting: loved ones, familiar routine, Internet access, and junk food. Blah blah blah. Things are hard enough as they are. If you're also having to face severe emotional distress, that makes things much worse.

During those ten days, I spent almost every one in intense emotional pain. I had nothing to do all day except to *try* to focus my attention on my breath. In other words, I couldn't do anything all day except to confront my unbearable emotional pain in the midst of physical discomfort. All day. Every day. Remarkably, about halfway into it, around day five, there was a twenty-five-hour period when my mind became effortlessly and intensely focused on the breath, and filled with deep calmness and relaxation, plus some degree of joy. It came out of nowhere, and in twenty-five hours, it completely disappeared. Weird. Outside of that time, though, I was on the Pain Channel: all pain, all day. I came out of the retreat thinking that 90 percent of it was a complete waste of my time. I hated it. I had far better things to do, thank you very much.

Tonight on the Pain Network:
a Duggar Family marathon!
Plus: The Real Housewives of Westeros!

When I returned to my regular life, however, I noticed a sudden transformation. For reasons I could not explain at the time, I was full of inner confidence. When my friends saw me, they all had the same reaction. They all asked some variation of, "What happened to you? You look great. You look so . . . confident."

When I reflected on it with my teacher, I figured out what had happened. Sometime after day two or so, I grew tired of fighting my emotional pain and overwhelming sense of failure, so I decided to just allow them to occupy my entire body and mind. Soon thereafter, I decided that I would also stop looking away from them. Instead, I'd look intently at them and **bear witness** to them. All those unpleasant sensations in the body involved in the emotionality of pain and feelings of failure, all those thoughts of unworthiness, even that awful self-talk that told me I was not even worthy of being alive, I just sat and bore witness to them. By this time, I was already a seasoned meditator, so I knew that I was supposed to look at all internal phenomena with equanimity and kindness, but in this case, the depth of my practice was not yet remotely capable of generating equanimity and kindness in the face of that much pain and failure, so all I could do was bear witness. Not with equanimity, not with kindness, just witnessing.

Today, with hindsight from the vantage point of a more matured practice, I can see that the key ingredient in my transformation was the **mere willingness** to bear witness to pain and suffering within myself. Just to be willing to do it was huge. Upon reflection, I realized that there is a word in the English language that denotes willingness to confront all things bad, and that word is: *courage.* Without knowing it at the time, I had spent those difficult days cultivating courage. At the end of it, what came out was a small but perceptible increase in my courage in the face of emotional pain. And that was what explained my sudden increase in confidence. It was the confidence of courage.

Meditation Makes You Attractive

Once, I was interviewed by a reporter doing a story on meditation. He asked me about the benefits of meditation, so I gave him a fairly long list: improves your health, reduces stress, increases emotional resilience, makes you a more effective leader, etc., etc., etc. The reporter threw up his hands and said, "Okay, is there anything that meditation does *not* improve?" I pointed to myself and said, "It doesn't make you sexy." We both laughed. But then when I reflected on it later, I realized I wasn't entirely right, because meditation can make you more attractive. How so? In a big 1995 study, more than 1,500 men and women from the United States, Russia, and Japan were asked what traits they most desire in marriage partners.[7] Among both men and women in all three very different cultures, the number one most desired trait is being "kind and understanding." In other words, **kindness is extremely attractive.** In addition, as we will see in Chapter 5, we know that kindness is highly trainable; therefore, you can train yourself to be a very attractive marriage partner by doing the practices in that chapter. (I can already imagine a bad TV ad for this book where a grinning man sitting in his bedroom tells the camera, "I did the exercises in this book, and my girlfriend thinks I'm a new man!")

LICENSED TO CHILL

There is another way meditation can make you more attractive, not just as a potential marriage partner but also to people you work with: **meditation can increase your charisma.** According to my dear friend and author of *The Charisma Myth*, Olivia Fox Cabane, charisma is the result of specific behaviors: behaviors of **presence,** behaviors of **power,** and behaviors of **warmth.**[8] All three are critical. Behaviors of power come from authentic self-confidence, and as we discussed in the preceding section, meditation can give you that kind of confidence.

Behaviors of presence, in my opinion, involve being totally here, in the present moment; and being totally *with* whomever you are interacting with. Mindfulness practice makes you good at being totally here. There's a nice story to illustrate being totally with, which is a short story by Tolstoy called "The Three Questions." The ultra-short version of that short story is this: A king decided that if he knew the answer to three questions, he would always do the right thing. And the three questions are: One, when is the most important time? Two, who is the most important person? Three, what is the most important thing to do? Eventually, he learned the answers from a wise man. The most important time is now, because now is the only time which you have some control over. The most important person is the person you're interacting with. The most important thing to do is to do your best to serve the person you are interacting with. Know these, the wise man told the king, and you will always do the right thing. In order to have strong presence, be in the present, treat the person you are interacting with as the most important person in the world, and do your best to serve him or her. The training for presence, therefore, is mindfulness (Chapters 2 and 3) and compassion (Chapter 5). Practice these two things and you will have a strong presence.

Behaviors of warmth, in my opinion, can be reduced to a single sentence: "I'm so happy to see you." If you meet somebody and tell yourself, "I am so happy to see this person," it shows up naturally in your face and in your body. So just by doing that, you will project warmth. The training for warmth is loving-kindness (Chapter 5). The stronger your loving-kindness practice, the more organically and effortlessly you can project warmth.

Hence, by practicing mindfulness, loving-kindness, and compassion, you will become more charismatic. That, and maybe everybody will want to marry you.

The Luck of the Happy

Mind training can make you lucky. (No, I'm not talking about "getting lucky"—that's the previous section, maybe).

A friend once asked me what the secret of my success is. I like to say I am successful because I am smart and hardworking, but that is not entirely true, because I know people who are smarter and harder working than I am who are not doing as well. Upon reflection, I realized the secret of my success can be encapsulated in a single word: *luck*. I am so successful because I am lucky.

Fortunately, luck is not completely random. I am blessed with three kinds of luck that led me to become successful, and of the three, only the first is completely random. I have some power over the other two, though of course, this being luck, there are no 100 percent guarantees. The three kinds of luck are:

1. Being born into the right circumstances

2. Being in the right place at the right time

3. Being surrounded by good people

1. Being Born into the Right Circumstances

I was born into a family that was poor but caring. In my entire life, I always had enough to eat (and I know my mom sometimes went hungry to ensure that). I always had shelter. I never suffered a single day of war nor a single day of homelessness. Despite being born in what was then a poor, developing country, my country had always given me clean water on tap, free vaccinations, and free education. Billionaire Warren Buffett famously referred to those who grow up in prosperity as "members of the lucky sperm club,"[9] and given the circumstances of my birth and growing up, I too consider myself a member of that club. There are many millions of people who are born into circumstances in which they do not even have access to books, much less to education or clean water. If you are reading this book, it is likely that you are blessed with at least the same luck I was.

I have not done a single thing to deserve this kind of luck—I am just lucky. The only thing I can do is pay it forward by committing to making the world a better place in my lifetime.

2. Being in the Right Place at the Right Time

This kind of luck is not completely random. We all have some power to contribute to it, and in my case I have done two things. One is to **always be prepared for opportunity** in case it arises. I always try to do my best, most outstanding work. When I was an intern at IBM in 1999, CEO Lou Gerstner took time to speak to the interns. One of my fellow interns asked him what had contributed most to his own success. He said it was always doing an outstanding job, no matter the work. Even if it's a thankless job, even if it's a task that offers no promotion prospects, always do outstanding work. If we do, eventually somebody will notice, and when a reliable person is needed for an important job, somebody will say, "How about that Lou guy? He always does outstanding work. Maybe we should give him a try." Lou said that is the story of his life, how he kept getting promoted to take on more and more responsibilities. This has turned out to be true in my experience.

Another way I prepare for opportunities is by constantly prioritizing my personal growth, sometimes with spectacular results. In early 2000, when I was looking for a job, it was the height of the dot-com boom, and anybody with a pulse and a software engineering degree could get a job in Silicon Valley. Being an award-winning software engineer with straight A's from a top university, I could have any job I wanted. I decided to join a small, unprofitable startup with a silly name called Google. Why? Because I decided I never want to be the smartest person in the room. If I am the smartest person in the room, I won't learn anything. Hence, to maximize my personal growth, I chose to work in a company where people seemed to be much smarter than I, and it was Google. And, boy, did that decision work out.

Then, I **bravely jump at opportunities** when they do arise. Taking advantage of big opportunities often requires us to make major transitions, and those can be scary. My dear friend Scott Kriens, the admired former CEO of Juniper Networks, compares it to flying between trapezes: there has to be a moment when you are willing to let go of a trapeze and be in midair without any support whatsoever. If you are not willing to do that, you will never be able to fly between trapezes. Taking advantage of major opportunities often requires completely letting go of something safe and comfortable, and venturing into a deeply uncomfortable unknown. Doing so takes two things: the self-confidence to put yourself in very uncomfortable situations, and the self-awareness to clearly know your values, priorities, and purpose in life.

In late 2007, when I was serving as an engineer in Google, I led the creation of the mindfulness-based emotional intelligence curriculum called Search Inside Yourself in my free time. A few months later, Google's People Operations department (which is what we call our human resources function) offered me a position to work on Search Inside Yourself full time. I would be the first practicing engineer in the history of Google to transfer into People Operations. In the engineering department, I was a respected, pioneering member with valuable skills that I had spent a lifetime honing, while in People Operations, I would be a questionable transplant who knew zilch about HR. At the not-so-tender age of thirty-seven, I would have to rebuild almost everything from scratch, including my professional skills, connections, credentials, and credibility. Well, of course I should have said no. However, I checked in on my values and decided that while I liked writing code, what really gave me purpose was scaling inner peace, inner joy, and compassion worldwide, and People Operations would provide me the opportunity to do so. And so I held my breath and flew between trapezes. By 2012, I would be internationally recognized as the person who popularized mindfulness at Google and thereby helped legitimize mindfulness in the corporate world. I think I made the right move.

In life, opportunity knocks fairly often, but if you are unprepared for it or unwilling to jump at it, then it will pass you by. That happens to many people. If, however, you are prepared for opportunities, you are always trying to grow and always doing your best, you are keenly aware of what gives you purpose, and you develop the courage to answer when opportunities turn up at your door, then you will be able to take advantage of them, and they will change your life, and the people around you will wonder why you are so frequently in the right place at the right time. In fact, you probably don't get any more opportunities than they do—the difference is you can and do take advantage of the ones you get. The skills you need to do this are the self-awareness that gives you clarity of purpose, the self-confidence to know you are capable of learning anything at any age, the resilience to do outstanding work even in unpleasant situations, and the courage to "fly between trapezes" and put yourself in uncomfortable situations. Every one of these skills can be improved with the mind training practices in this book.

3. Being Surrounded by Good People

My success depends on being constantly surrounded by good people who want to help me. For example, when I needed help with my meditation practice, some of the greatest Western meditation teachers such as Jack Kornfield and Shinzen Young offered to personally tutor me, despite their busy schedules. When my team was designing Search Inside Yourself, amazing folks like Daniel Goleman (who literally wrote the book on emotional intelligence) offered their advice and assistance. When I needed to form a volunteer team at Google to work on the One Billion Acts of Peace campaign (which was later nominated for the Nobel Peace Prize by Archbishop Desmond Tutu and six other Nobel Laureates), a hundred people volunteered. I stand on the shoulders of many giants. I am successful only because so many good-hearted, outstanding, and capable people have given me so much help. I am lucky to always be the recipient of their kindness and generosity.

Once again, I find that my good luck on this front is not completely random. Three things helped tremendously. The first is genuinely loving people. I do that by treating everybody I meet with loving-kindness. Another thing that helps is earning the respect of people. I do this by behaving with integrity, honoring commitments with outstanding work, and practicing self-confidence based on equanimity. Perhaps the most important thing is to constantly aspire to serve the greater good. If you always try to practice compassion and you are always trying to benefit the people around you and beyond, the good people around you will love you and want to help you.

Essentially, this third aspect of luck comes most from loving-kindness and compassion. Fortunately, both are highly trainable and are described in detail in Chapter 5.

We have all heard the expression "We make our own luck." Unfortunately, people sometimes take this to mean that if someone is unlucky, it is their own fault. This is not how luck works. If we could control every aspect of our luck, we wouldn't need the word. However, many qualities we can train—such as self-knowledge, confidence, courage, loving-kindness, and compassion—can greatly increase our luck. These qualities also all come with the territory of joy. Thus, if you do the trainings in this book, you will not only experience more joy, but you will also improve your luck. That, I can guarantee.

Hopefully by now you're so excited about the multiple benefits of mind training that you can't wait to read the rest of this book. I know I'm excited for you, here at the beginning of this joyful journey. Nothing less than calm, clarity, emotional resilience, self-awareness, creativity, confidence, kindness, charisma, luck, and yes, joy await you in the chapters to come.

CHAPTER TWO

Just One Breath?
Surely You Jest

How Joy Can Begin with the First Breath

If mind training is so good, why isn't everybody doing it daily?

One difficulty with mind training is that it can be very hard to start. Another difficulty is, even when successfully initiated, it can be very hard to sustain. Fortunately, I think these problems are highly solvable.

Let's again use the analogy of exercise. Everybody knows that exercise is good for us. Every man, for example, wants to have Fabio's body (I'm guessing many women want to have Fabio's body too, but in a different way). There is a simple reason not every man has Fabio's body: it's really hard to get into such amazing shape. It takes thousands of hours of hard training, and most of us men dislike that training much more than we dislike our current un-Fabio-like bodies. Fortunately, we don't need to look like Fabio to enjoy many of the wonderful benefits of physical fitness—all we need is twenty minutes of exercise three times a week to gain the type of physical fitness we need to change our lives. Sadly, even that is hard for very many people.

Every year, some large number of people have New Year's resolutions to start exercising. Many start going to the gym or jogging. After some days or weeks, some people just give up, usually with sore bodies. Those who persist will find their bodies being conditioned to exercise. After two weeks or so, their bodies are no longer sore, and after about week seven or eight, they find their exercise beginning to have life-changing effects. They're healthier, they have more energy, they look better, and they feel great about themselves. And then what happens? Some number of months later, some large percentage begin to exercise less and less. Their exercise regimens start to taper off. Why? Because they have "no time." It's boring, it's tedious, it's hard work, and they're too busy, or tired, or something.

I know it's healthy, but after a
while, I just couldn't see where
it was all going.

What to do? There are at least two obvious solutions. The first is community. Simply, if you have people to exercise with, for example gym buddies or running buddies, then you're more likely to do it. The second solution is incorporating exercise into daily life. For example, instead of driving to work, you choose to bike to work, so the daily commute becomes daily exercise. Or, for the less gung-ho types, you take the stairs rather than the elevator, so you get some exercise during the workday (which is probably easier here in low-rise Silicon Valley than in most of Manhattan).

There is, however, a third, less obvious but most important solution: joy.

There are two parts to incorporating joy into exercise. The first is a skillful ramp-up, which means that at the beginning, you put the trainee onto the exercise regimen skillfully. At this stage, the key is **easing into it, skillfully.** The skillful trainer doesn't work the trainee too hard at first because this tends to provoke psychological resistance to the training, but at the same time, the training cannot be so easy that it has no meaningful impact. The trainer must understand the minimum effective dose of exercise and train at an intensity that is slightly higher but not too much higher than the minimum effective dose. This makes training both easy and effective at the beginning; the trainee eases into the exercise and gradually ramps up. More than anything, this requires proper understanding of the training process.

The second part of incorporating joy into exercise is **making it fun.** If you can make exercise fun, then people will do it, and they will never have "no time" because people will always make time for fun. There is a word that encapsulates this solution: *sports*. People play tennis, basketball, and other sports because they have fun doing so, and in having fun, they get exercise. If sports were invented by us engineers, we would have called it "gamified exercise."

In other words, the solution to sustaining an exercise routine is to make it joyful, through skillful application of ease and fun.

In my experience, we have similar problems in training the mind, and they can be solved with similar solutions. Each year, people hear about those wondrous benefits of meditation, and many decide to give it a try. After some days or weeks, many people just give up, thinking it's too hard. Those who get the hang of it and persist for a while will find their training begins to have life-changing effects. They're calmer, more focused, happier, and kinder, and they feel great about themselves. And then what happens? Some number of months later, some large percentage see their practice start to taper off. Why? Because they have "no time." It's boring, it's tedious, it's hard work, and they're too busy, or tired, or something.

All three solutions for sustaining an exercise routine also work for sustaining a meditation practice. Historically, people have used community, meditating together and supporting each other's practice. This hasn't seemed to work very well in the modern context. I think part of the reason is that, for meditation to work really well, it's good to practice around twenty minutes a day, and in modern society it's hard to gather your buddies for twenty minutes a day for anything that doesn't involve beer. Incorporating practice into daily life is also a common solution. We call them "informal practices," such as walking to the bathroom mindfully, or taking mindful breaths while waiting for the computer to start up. Informal practices are very beneficial, but in my experience, they can only complement formal sitting practice, not replace it, because they lack the rigor of formal sitting practice. It's like trying to develop stamina by taking walks in the park. Walking in the park is good for your health, but not sufficiently rigorous for developing stamina.

That means we need to rely strongly on joy as the solution, just as we do for exercise.

There is a point in every meditator's practice that I imaginatively call the Joy Point. This is the point where the meditator gains reliable access to inner peace and inner joy, at least during meditation. The reason is, when a meditator's practice reaches a sufficient depth, she can access inner peace on demand, at least during sitting meditation, and that inner peace creates the conditions for the arising of inner joy. Therefore, with enough training, she is also able to access inner joy on demand. There's a caveat, which is that some people experience the joy aspect more strongly than peace and some may experience the peace aspect more strongly than joy, so there may be some disagreement about which aspect is stronger, but what is clear is that both are present. I decided to call it the Joy Point rather than the Peace and Joy Point because I'm too lazy to type that much.

The most important thing about this is **self-sustaining momentum.** Once a person hits the Joy Point, the virtuous cycle of joy and skillfulness keeps her going. She has the skill to reliably access inner peace and inner joy, which makes her practice joyful, so she practices more and becomes more skillful, which makes her practice more joyful, and so on. This is the point where she stops complaining to the author of *Search Inside Yourself* that she cannot sustain her meditation practice.

Hence, the key question we must ask is, how do we accelerate toward the Joy Point? In thinking about the problem, I realized that the solution is not to accelerate toward joy but instead to *frontload* joy in the process of mind training. This means introducing joy from the beginning rather than waiting to discover it at some point years from now—and risking that we don't get to that point. Better still, the joy/meditation virtuous cycle can be kick-started with very little effort: as little as one hundred minutes of practice (about the time it takes to watch *Frozen*, fly from San Francisco to Las Vegas, or make a pie from scratch), which we will explore in this chapter.

Don't Worry, Be Lazy

Be not afraid of laziness: some are born lazy, some achieve laziness, and some have laziness thrust upon them.

The first step in applying joy to meditation is easing. This is where you ease into practice and arrive at the realization that meditation does not have to be hard. In fact, it can actually be quite easy. As you settle into ease, a sense of joy arises that is born of ease, and when abiding in that joy, the mind relaxes some more and ease becomes more firmly established, thus creating a virtuous cycle. This is how easing is the first step to establishing and applying joy in meditation. How do we begin to establish this ease? With laziness, of course. Not just any laziness, but wise laziness.

At Google, where I spent most of my engineering career, we hire some of the best engineers in the world. I say half-jokingly that I like to hire engineers who are lazy, because lazy engineers always find the most efficient way to do things. For that to work, however, they must be lazy in a very specific way. These engineers must be highly motivated and proficient, they care about producing high-quality results, but they are too lazy to do unnecessary work, so they take the time to gain thorough insights into a system in order to find the easiest way to accomplish what they need.

This is wise laziness. Using insight and wisdom to maximize ease without sacrificing quality of results, thereby benefiting yourself and all others who come after you. I like to apply wise laziness to the process of mind training, mostly because I'm striving very hard to be lazy.

How Long Before I Get the Benefits?

Many beginners ask one important question about meditation that seldom gets properly answered. That question is, "How long do I have to practice before I start to see meaningful benefits?" In my experience, the answer given by teachers is almost always some variation of, "Don't think about it, just sit." When I was a beginner, I was frequently annoyed by that non-answer. Why don't they just tell it to us straight? In hindsight, I think one reason was because they believed it'd take a discouragingly long time, so they didn't want us to be looking out for the goal. I imagine they especially didn't want to tell me the answer because they were too kind to say to me, "Maybe one year, but for you, Meng, ten years."

I learned that many people, teachers and students alike, make the assumption that meditation takes a long time to bring about meaningful benefits. This assumption probably has cultural origins, because over the past few thousand years, meditation was taught and practiced in cultures where almost all meditators practiced full time for years. Therefore, meditation training programs were optimized for full-time practitioners with lots of free time and not much else to do, and they were designed for arriving at nothing less than profound mastery over the mind. Because that target audience and use case had not changed in thousands of years, everybody assumed that meditation necessarily requires long periods of rigorous practice over many years, and nobody questioned that assumption. Nobody, that is, until lazy engineers like me with a chronic shortage of free time started learning meditation. What is one of the most important (and annoying) things highly effective engineers do? We question assumptions.

The first crack in the assumption for me came from observing that many participants in mindfulness-based courses such as Mindfulness-Based Stress Reduction (MBSR) and Search Inside Yourself (SIY) report their lives changing during the short seven or eight weeks of their training. Based on that, I did a rough tally and arrived at the conclusion that it takes no more than a hundred hours of practice before a meditator begins to experience benefits that are significant enough to be life changing. After that, whenever people asked me how long they had to meditate before it begins to change their life, I would say, "About a hundred hours." These days, however, I say, "About fifty to a hundred hours." Why? Because I found out that when the Dalai Lama was asked a similar question, he said, "About fifty hours." I had to adjust my answer so that the Dalai Lama and I can both be correct at the same time.

I was in for a much bigger surprise. It turns out that benefits are available well below the fifty-hours mark. A 2007 study by Chinese scientist Y. Y. Tang showed that a hundred minutes of meditation training is sufficient to effect measurable changes.[1] One hundred minutes! Not ten thousand hours, not a hundred hours, not even two hours. Wow. A much more recent, 2013 study reinforced the hundred-minutes finding.[2] In this study, students who practiced mindfulness meditation for ten minutes a day for two weeks, a total of 140 minutes, had measurably improved GRE scores. Yes, just two hours and twenty minutes to improve your GRE scores. I can already see Asian "tiger moms" rushing to enroll their kids in mindfulness meditation classes after they read the preceding sentence.

But wait, who needs 140 minutes when you can derive benefit in only fifteen minutes? Another 2013 study shows that a mere fifteen minutes of mindfulness meditation can measurably improve your decision making by reducing your vulnerability to something called the sunk-cost bias, which contributes to bad decisions (like going to a movie you don't actually want to see because you bought a non-refundable ticket).[3]

It gets better. It turns out that mind training can affect changes even at the epigenetic level in a surprisingly short amount of time. A groundbreaking 2013 study by my dear friend and pioneer in contemplative neuroscience Richard "Richie" Davidson showed that when experienced meditators spent eight hours in intensive mindfulness practice, their gene expression started to change.[4] Specifically, there was a reduction in the expression of pro-inflammatory genes, which correlates with faster physical recovery from a stressful situation. Jaw-dropping stuff.

Given all these data points and the experience of participants in my Search Inside Yourself classes, I arrived at a belief that meditative skills may be developed at rates comparable to skills for other complex activities. Take piano playing for example. It takes maybe one or two hours to learn to play a very simple song. Once you can play a simple song, you have the experience of making music. Yay! True, you only know how to play a single song, but that is a meaningful, objectively measurable improvement in your music-making abilities. To go beyond one song, however, to be able to play some small number of simple songs, takes a significantly larger number of hours, maybe fifty to a hundred. At that point, you cannot claim to be good at this, but at least you can now tell yourself that you can play the piano. To be very good, however, takes a much larger number of hours. Perhaps after one or two thousand hours of practice, you become very good at the piano, good enough to be invited to play in your local church regularly, or to be asked to teach your neighbor's kids. Finally, to gain mastery, for example, to be good enough to play professionally with a symphony orchestra, it takes a very large number of hours of practice. Author Malcolm Gladwell reports the number is ten thousand hours, and I suspect this is likely correct. In either case, it takes many years of practice to get there.

I believe the numbers are comparable for training in meditation. To learn enough of the basics to derive meaningful benefit, akin to learning to play a simple song on the piano, takes some fairly small number of minutes to a very small number of hours. The research, as I mentioned earlier, suggests roughly fifteen minutes to two hours to experience benefits (depending on the benefit—some take more practice than others). But that is not enough for meditation to start changing your life. For it to begin to change your life takes fifty to a hundred hours. At that point, your practice is good enough that you can quite often taste the sweetness of peace and joy in your sitting, or you start to become resilient in the face of painful experiences, and you see your practice begin to affect your daily life. For some people, this experience is life changing; for others, they at least understand how meditation can change their lives. To become very good at meditation, good enough, for example, that you are able to access peace and joy in sitting meditation about 95 to 99 percent of the time in normal circumstances, and good enough for you to calm your mind in difficult situations more than half the time, takes about one thousand to two thousand hours of practice. This is the reason why I want all Search Inside Yourself teachers to have at least two thousand hours of lifetime meditation practice; I don't need all of them to be masters, but I need them to at least be very good. To be a master of meditation takes many thousands of hours of practice. I don't know the exact number, ten thousand sounds like a reasonable estimate to me, but I also know it is a very rough estimate with a lot of variance.

The key point is, meditation takes a long time to master, but it is very easy to learn and it takes only a short amount of time for meditation to start changing your life. In that sense, meditation obeys an aphorism called Bushnell's Law, named after Nolan Bushnell, founder of the video games company Atari. Bushnell's Law states, "All the best games are easy to learn and difficult to master."

This leads us to a question only a shamelessly lazy engineer would ask: what is the absolute minimum amount of meditation practice before there is any sort of benefit? My answer: one breath.

Just One Breath? Surely You Can't Be Serious

I am serious. And don't call me Shirley.[5] Here, try it right now. It doesn't get easier than this, I promise.

You called?

Sorry, Shirley! False alarm!

FORMAL PRACTICE: ONE MINDFUL BREATH

You may close your eyes or keep them open. Take one slow, deep breath. For the duration of that one breath, **give your full attention to your breath in a gentle way.** Total and gentle attention on feeling your breath, that is all. If you prefer a more specific instruction, bring attention to the feeling in either your nose or your belly as you breathe.

When I guide this exercise in a classroom setting, I like to joke that all participants just earned themselves new bragging rights: they just spent an *entire* meditation session without losing their attention on even a single breath. Jokes aside, though, notice that already you are likely to be a little calmer and more relaxed after the breath than before it. You already gain some benefit with the very first breath.

There are two reasons, one physiological and one psychological, why taking that one mindful breath induces calmness and relaxation. The physiological reason is that breaths taken mindfully tend to be slow and deep, and taking slow, deep breaths stimulates the vagus nerve, which in turn activates the parasympathetic nervous system. That lowers stress, reduces your heart rate and blood pressure, and basically calms you down. The psychological reason is that when you put your attention intensely on the breath, you are fully in the present for the duration of the breath. To feel regretful, you need to be in the past, and to worry, you need to be in the future. Hence, when you are fully in the present, you are temporarily free from regret and worry. Carrying regret and worry is like hauling a heavy burden, and to be temporarily free from regret and worry, even for the duration of just one breath, is like temporarily putting down the burden. It allows the body and mind to enjoy a precious moment of rest and recovery.

The ability to rest and recover may have game-changing consequences for you, sometimes literally. A friend of mine who is an avid tennis player tells me that one very important thing that distinguishes the best tennis players in the world is their ability to reset and calm down their bodies and minds in the ten to fifteen seconds between points. When the next point begins, they are in a more restful state than they were at the end of the previous point. Because of this, they can sustain high performance over and over again, which is how they win the Grand Slams. I found that insight fascinating, but for a long time I could not verify it because I had no access to the best tennis players in the world. And then one day, I had the fortune to meet Novak Djokovic, one of the very best tennis players in the history of the game. The first question I asked him was whether the above claim is true. He confirmed that it is indeed true. More than that, he said that at his level, tennis is no longer a physical game—it is a mental game, and a key part of that mental game is the ability to stay calm whatever happens.

If you ever aspire to become one of the best tennis players in the history of the game, you know what to do.

Gentle and Intense

Simply taking one mindful breath under any circumstances is beneficial. However, for those wishing to optimize its benefits, for that one breath to work very well, it is good to have generous helpings of two key ingredients: **gentleness in attitude,** and **intensity of attention.**

Attending with intensity and gentleness is like gazing at your baby or the way your puppy looks at you. The attention is intense but also gentle and effortless. The idea is to bring the same intensity and gentleness to the object of meditation, in this case, the breath. A traditional analogy is holding a small bird in your hand (which may or may not be worth two in the bush, but I digress). Your grasp is gentle enough that you don't kill the bird; at the same time, it is firm and intense enough to keep the bird from flying away.

Gentleness comes naturally to some people, but if it doesn't come naturally to you, don't worry. There are three qualities you can use, any one of which can help you get there. The first is **physical relaxation.** Put yourself in a situation that is physically relaxing for you. For example, sit in your favorite chair, go for a jog, or take a bath. When you feel relaxed, pay attention to this feeling so that your mind becomes familiar with it. Where there is relaxation, gentleness follows. The second quality is the sense of **mental ease.** Remember that meditation can be easy. You're not doing anything in particular, you are simply noticing the breath, which happens by itself anyway. Even better, you are doing it only for the duration of a single breath. It's so easy, even Meng can do it. There is nowhere to go, nothing to do, no goal to achieve. Where there is a sense of ease, gentleness follows. The third quality is **loving-kindness.** The reason gazing at your baby is so effortless is because love and kindness are both involved. See if there is any way you can bring up loving-kindness, by applying it either to yourself, to the experience of the breath, or to the present moment. Alternatively, call up a memory involving an abundance of loving-kindness and enjoy that memory before doing the One Mindful Breath meditation. When the mind is immersed in loving-kindness, gentleness follows.

Intensity is important because the more intensely you are attending to the present moment, the more temporary freedom you gain from regrets about the past and worries about the future. Furthermore, the more intensely you practice, the longer the benefits linger after the practice. Tibetan masters compare it to very strong perfume. If you have a small bottle of very intense perfume, if you open the cap for even just a few seconds, the fragrance will linger in the room for a long time. Similarly, whether you are practicing concentration, calmness, present-moment attention, or loving-kindness, the more intensely you can bring it up, the longer it will linger and benefit you.

There is an observation in the field of sports science that provides
a dramatic demonstration of the power of intensity—in this case,
physical training. It comes from a form of training called High-
Intensity Interval Training (HIIT).

One particular HIIT training regimen called the Timmons regimen (named after Jamie Timmons, a professor of systems biology
at the University of Loughborough) was illustrated on a BBC documentary program called "The Truth About Exercise."[6] In this documentary, two subjects were shown. One subject biked at a speed
he could sustain for thirty minutes a day. The other biked intensely
for merely one minute a day, going all out for twenty seconds until
he was exhausted, resting for a few minutes, and then going all out
again. He did this three times, for a total training time of one minute.
Weeks later, they both achieved the same improvements in at least
two important measures: VO_2 max, the amount of oxygen the body
is capable of utilizing, and insulin sensitivity, which measures how
sensitive the body is to the effects of insulin. One minute versus thirty
minutes, both achieving the same improvements. Wow. I am a practitioner of the Timmons regimen myself, and it appears to have worked
very well for me. I apply the same principle to my daily meditation: at
least some fraction of my daily meditation involves intense attention
to my breath.

A high level of intensity in meditation is when the object of meditation, in this case the breath, occupies all your foreground attention. The mind may be aware of other phenomena, such as thoughts,
sounds, or images, but they are all in the background. In the foreground of attention, there is nothing but the breath.

There is a Zen story that illustrates a very high level of attentional
intensity. A Zen master asked his students, "How long is one lifetime?" The students volunteered a variety of answers, "Fifty years."
"Seventy years." "One hundred years." To each answer, the master

replied, "No." Finally, when the room went silent, the master said, "Monks, remember this: a lifetime is the period between two breaths."

In response to this story, one of my friends, an admired Buddhist meditation teacher herself, joked, "Yes, the period between the very first breath and the very last breath." (It is true, advanced Buddhist meditators are a humorous bunch, up to and including the Dalai Lama.)

Jokes aside, the story gives you an idea of attention so intense that it is as if all of life experience is right here, in this one present moment. The moment feels almost timeless because when the mind is so strongly in the present that past and future are merely concepts, the only experience is here and now. That experience does not require ten thousand hours of training—it can be tasted here and now, for the duration of one breath. We can all already do it without training. What ten thousand hours of training does is enable the mind to concentrate this way for however long it wants at whatever depth it chooses, effortlessly. But the basic qualitative experience is already available to all of us.

It is imperative that we apply gentleness at the same time as intensity. In other words, if intensity comes at the cost of gentleness, then it is not a price worth paying. For example, if being intensely focused on the breath causes you to feel stressed out, then you must lower the intensity until you no longer feel stressed. Here is an important general rule: if, for whatever reason, you can only choose one, **always choose gentleness over intensity.** In this case, attend very gently to the breath, and over time, as you become accustomed to gentleness and get comfortably relaxed with the breath, then increase intensity.

Make Breathing a Habit

One of the best things about the One Mindful Breath practice is that since it is so easy and takes so little time, you can practice anytime and anywhere. In geek speak, I say it is highly portable. That's the good news. The better news is, by its nature, it can be turned into a habit very easily. According to Charles Duhigg, author of *The Power of Habit,* a habit is a loop that consists of three parts: a cue, a routine, and a reward.[7] The cue is something that activates the habit—it leads to the routine. The routine is the behavior itself—it leads to the reward. The reward is the perceived benefit that comes from doing the behavior, and it reinforces the habit so that the next occurrence of the same cue is more likely to automatically activate the routine. Thus a loop forms. One example of this habit loop is brushing my teeth twice a day. There are two cues for me: getting out of bed in the morning and getting ready for bed at night. When those cues happen, I automatically—almost without thinking—walk to my bathroom to activate the routine, which is the actual brushing of my teeth. The reward is the sensation and satisfaction associated with clean teeth.

In the case of doing one mindful breath, the routine is to bring attention to the next breath (and, when possible, a gentle and intense attention). The reward is the sense of calmness that comes from the routine. All you need is the cue. Once you find the right cue, you will be able to form a habit loop and you will have at least a few breaths per day of meditation you can benefit from, which I promise you is far better than zero.

There are a number of cues you can consider. You can use the first moment of your day as your cue. The moment you wake up, take one mindful breath and know that you have just been given the gift of another day to live. You can also use the moment you lie down in bed at night as your cue, in which case the mindful breath relaxes you in preparation for a good night's sleep. Or you can add an hourly chime to your watch or smartphone and get a mindful breath once each waking hour. These are all great cues, and I use all of them. The one I most highly recommend, however, is this: **every time you have to wait, take a mindful breath.** I spend a lot of my time waiting, and I imagine you do too. I wait at traffic stops and at lunch queues. I wait at the airport, at the train station, and at the taxi stand. I wait for meetings to begin, for VIPs to arrive, for my computer to start up, for webpages to load up. So much waiting. Every time I need to wait, I take one or more mindful breaths.

This is a wonderful practice with many benefits. First, I never waste any time anymore, because every moment I wait is a moment I get to spend productively, practicing mindfulness meditation. Second, if the waiting causes me any agitation, I get to use the breath to calm down. And perhaps best of all, once you do this practice often enough that it becomes a habit, you will never be bored anymore because boredom itself becomes a cue. At the first sign of boredom, the mind goes like, "Yay! I get to meditate." And then the mind just spontaneously engages in meditation. No more boredom.

Actually, there are exceptions. For myself, in the past ten years or so, I can remember exactly two times I was bored. One was near the end of a ten-day meditation retreat when I was so tired with practice, I temporarily lost my ability to meditate for a day, and during that day, I experienced boredom. Another time was when I was in an audience watching an extremely bad stage production. It was so bad, I could not bear to watch another minute of it, but it was so loud, I could not drop into meditation at the time, so I was bored. However, in the first case, I was suffering despair, and in the second case, agitation, so both times, I was suffering from something far more intense than boredom, hence boredom itself wasn't really a problem. Therefore, the number of times in the past ten years or so when boredom per se was a real problem for me: zero. I have found this to be a common experience among seasoned meditators.

This is yet another cool benefit of mind training: you will suffer less boredom until, with practice, you reach a point where you will very seldom, almost never, experience boredom again for the rest of your life.

Even more important, once the cue-routine-reward cycle of one mindful breath is strongly established, it's a mental habit, and with this habit, very soon, the mind gets familiarized with meditation. Through familiarization, formal meditation practice becomes both easier to do and easier to sustain. All that, plus all those one breaths add up over time. This practice yields benefits here and now, it yields even greater benefits in the future, and it takes almost no extra time. Life doesn't get much easier than this.

INFORMAL PRACTICE: CREATING A HABIT OF TAKING MINDFUL BREATHS

Choose a cue, something that, when it occurs, activates the habit of taking a mindful breath. The cue I most highly recommend is any situation when you have to wait.

Whenever the cue occurs, take one slow, deep breath and bring some amount of attention to that breath. For safety reasons (for example, if you're walking or driving), you may need to maintain an appropriate amount of attention to your surroundings as you pay some attention to your breath.

If taking that mindful breath makes you feel any better, simply notice that. It will be the reward that reinforces the habit.

Joy Starts Here, with the First Breath

At this point in your practice, after you have done some iterations of one mindful breath, you may already begin to taste a tiny hint of the joy of practice. It may be too subtle at this time for you to consciously notice it; in which case, it is fine because as your practice deepens, the joy will get stronger and your ability to perceive it will also get sharper, so it is only a matter of time before the joy of practice becomes perceptible.

At this point, you may experience joy from any of four sources, two of which are short-lived and two of which are very important and highly durable.

The two short-lived sources of joy are the joy of novelty and the joy of perceived agency. The joy of novelty is the excitement of experiencing something new, which obviously fades away very quickly because, by definition, things don't stay new for very long. The joy of perceived agency is discovering that what you initially thought was totally beyond your control is something you can make some choices about. That joy is also short-lived because we habituate to it very quickly.

To me, the best illustration of these two sources of joy came from a little baby girl. One day, when my daughter was about three months old, shortly after she gained control of her own hands and fingers, I gave her a toy car for the first time and showed her how to play with it (by pushing it forward). She watched the demonstration with fascination, as if Daddy was the coolest guy on earth. She picked up the car, pushed it forward to see it move, and then she burst into laughter, as if that was the most amazing thing she had ever done in her life (which it probably was at the time, since her repertoire at that point mostly had to do with the processes surrounding ingestion and digestion). And then she did it a second time, picked up the car, pushed it forward, and burst out laughing. And a third time, and so on. It went on for a few minutes, after which the laughter faded. The fascination with the car lasted a few more minutes. I conjectured that my daughter had just experienced the joys of novelty (a toy car that can be made to move) and perceived agency (discovering that she could make a choice to cause the toy car to move). Of course, I could only conjecture since three-month-old babies do not usually engage in analytical discussions involving the subtleties of their mental states.

Adults can also experience the joys of novelty and perceived agency, but for us, the experience is extremely muted compared to babies because we sort of take agency for granted ("Hey look, I can move a small object from point A to point B, big deal.") and things usually have to be fairly intense to trigger a novelty response in us. Still, it is possible that we may experience a hint of these joys in doing mindful breathing, especially if we were somewhat agitated before the mindful breath and then became meaningfully calmer after it. There may be a novelty feeling of "Whoa, cool, I wasn't expecting that." And there may be a realization of agency, knowing that "There is actually something I can do to reduce my agitation in a very short amount of time, wow." Knowing that you are not entirely at the mercy of agitation can bring some joy.

However, even if you experience joy from both sources, they will be very short-lived, so let me tell you about two others I have found to be very important and highly sustainable. How sustainable? Twenty-plus years of meditation practice later, I still experience these kinds of joy a lot, and I expect to for the rest of my life. The first highly sustainable source of joy is the **joy of momentary relief from affliction.** The mind is very often in some state of affliction. Sometimes, the mind suffers from debilitating affliction such as despair, depression, or hatred. Quite often, it suffers from potent but not necessarily debilitating affliction such as greed, worry, remorse, fear, envy, or anger. Very often, even in the absence of more acute affliction, there is some subtle affliction such as low-level restlessness and agitation. Attending gently and intensely to one breath, we find some temporary relief from affliction, and consequently joy arises with that relief. This relief and joy are available starting from the first mindful breath. With practice, they can expand in both depth and time. In other words, relief and joy can increase in power to counter stronger and stronger afflictions for longer and longer durations. We will take another look in Chapter 4 when we talk about the joy of not being in pain.

The second highly sustainable source of joy is the **joy of ease.** This is something you may experience when you're sitting in a hot tub, in a state of alertness (not dozing off) and relaxation at the same time. In a hot tub there is, of course, joy from sensual pleasure, but in addition to and mostly independent of that, there is the joy of ease. Part of this joy of ease comes from the ease of the situation, that there is nothing particularly difficult to do at the moment, and the other part comes from being at ease with oneself. In my experience, the joy of ease is always available when the mind is both **alert and relaxed** at the same time. That has profound implications because "alert and relaxed" is precisely the description of the most basic meditative state. Therefore, as you learn more and more reliably to bring the mind to the basic meditative state, you also gain more and more reliable access to the joy of ease. Even better, with enough practice, this joy can grow in strength until it appears to envelope one's entire domain of experience. It is a gentle joy that appears to fill one's entire being.

The preceding paragraph leads us to a mind-shattering, life-altering conclusion, which is that with sufficient proficiency in nothing more than the most basic meditative state, one may gain **the ability to reliably access a highly sustainable source of gentle joy,** joy that is deep enough to appear to fill one's entire being. Yes, my friends, it is a big claim, and I am boldly making it. (I know we are only at Chapter 2—I promise this is not the climax of the book.) As we have seen, you already have this ability. With practice, you'll gain reliability, the "on demand" part of joy on demand. In my case, it took me very many hours of practice to gain this level of proficiency, but you may be able to do it in less time because you have begun this training with a much better understanding of the process than I had when I started.

The Stupidest Advice Gopi Has Ever Received Came from Me

I have a dear friend named Gopi Kallayil. Gopi is best known as the Google employee (called a Googler) who started the group called Yoglers, Googlers who practice yoga. He is also known as the Googler who orchestrated the first Google Hangouts meeting between the Dalai Lama and Archbishop Desmond Tutu, but that is another story.

Convinced of the many benefits of meditation, Gopi aspired to meditate for an hour a day but hadn't succeeded at doing so. One day, he asked me for advice. How could he manage to meditate for one hour a day, he asked. I said, "Easy, just commit to one breath a day. Anything after that one breath is bonus." Gopi gave me a look that said, "You're <expletive> kidding me, right?" He thought, "This is the stupidest thing I have ever heard in my life," but he didn't tell me that until a few years later. At that moment, all he said was, "Really?" (Of course, if had he said, "Surely you can't be serious," I would have said, "I am serious. And don't call me Shirley.")

I explained to him, "First, remember that meditation is mental training. That means the intention to do that one breath is itself a meditation, because every time that intention arises, your mind inclines toward doing meditation practice a little bit more. Therefore, even just having that daily intention alone is useful. Furthermore, one mindful breath is so easy and takes so little time, you have no excuse not to do it. You can say you don't have ten minutes today to meditate, but you cannot say you have no time for one breath, so making it a daily practice is extremely doable. Once you do one breath a day, you will generate momentum for your practice, and when the day arrives that you are ready to do long sits, the momentum is there for you."

Gopi respected me enough that even though it was *the* stupidest thing he had ever heard in his life, he gave it a try, just because I said so. But he didn't just start with one breath. He started with ten breaths a day (which takes about one minute) because he is an over-achiever and wanted to do ten times more than I asked. So he did ten breaths a day for a few days, and then he realized something very important. He realized that one hour of sitting is simply a lot of one breaths stringed next to each other—that's all. Over time, his daily sits got longer and longer, and within a few months, he succeeded in his goal of meditating for one hour a day.

Remember, my friends, never underestimate the power of one breath. Mental fitness and joy on demand both start here, with one breath.

CHAPTER THREE

From One Breath
to One Googol

Settling into Sustainable Joy

Pretend that you are a poor, starving, landless peasant in ancient India. One day, the king announces that he is opening the doors of the royal treasury and anybody can take as many coins as they want from it. There is only one condition: you may only take what you can personally carry.

Free coins! If you are wise, you will take at least a little bit of it. You may take one coin, and you can feed your family for a few days. This is good, but why stop at one coin? If you take two handfuls of coins, then you can feed your family for months. Even better, if you take the time to repair your pockets so that when you reach the royal treasury, you can stuff your pockets with coins in addition to those you can hold in your hands, then maybe you can buy a small farm and feed your family for life. Even better, if you take the time to make yourself a strong sack, then you can come home with a sack full of coins and you can be rich for life. Even better, if you also tell all your friends and family about it, so that all of them can benefit as well, you can increase your family and community wealth.

Doing only the One Mindful Breath practice is like taking only one coin from the royal treasury—you are wise to do it and you will derive immediate meaningful benefit, but with just a little more effort, you could have benefited much more, so not getting more is a huge wasted opportunity. Doing a hundred minutes of meditation practice is like grabbing two handfuls of coins—it's a big improvement for only a little effort, but still, you can gain even more. Accumulating fifty to a hundred hours of meditation practice is like repairing your pockets and stuffing them with the royal coins. It takes some effort, but you will begin to change your life. Accumulating thousands of hours of meditation practice is like going to the royal treasury with a strong sack. Yes, you will need to spend time and effort making a sack, and yes, you will exert a lot of effort carrying all those coins back home, but you will derive lifelong benefits beyond your wildest expectations. Finally, teaching the path to others is like telling all your family and friends about the king giving away his coins. You elevate all toward peace, joy, and goodness, and all of society benefits.

The fruits of meditation practice are like free coins, they are available to all who want them, and have been for the past thousands of years. The only thing one has to do is to get them. They have been independently rediscovered in one form or another in all faith traditions, and they are now also available in the secular world. I hope to see the vast majority of humanity filling pockets, sacks, wheelbarrows, and pickup trucks with meditation practice.

In this chapter, let us explore ways to skillfully extend the ease of our practices from one single breath to a fortune.

The Basic Training: Settling the Mind

Sometimes, you get lucky in life, when the most important thing you need to do turns out to also be the simplest. One example is breathing. Breathing is the most important thing we need to do in our lives, and for most of us, it is also the easiest thing we ever do. If you belong to the population of people who can breathe effortlessly, you are so lucky! The same turns out to be true for meditation, that the simplest skill in meditation is also the most important. What is it?

The simplest, most fundamental, most basic, and most important meditative skill of all is **the ability to settle the mind.**

What does it mean to settle the mind? Pretend you have a snow globe that you are constantly shaking. If I ask you to settle the snow globe, what do you do? You put it on the table, or the floor, or any other stationary surface. One of the literal meanings of the word settle is "to come down onto a surface." You literally settle the snow globe down, that is all. So easy. Once the snow globe is settled, then over time, the water in it becomes still, the snowflakes fall to the bottom, and the snow globe becomes calm and clear at the same time.

Settling the mind is similar. To settle the mind simply means resting it so that it approaches some degree of stillness. There are many ways to settle the mind, but I like to suggest three methods that are easy and highly effective.

The first method is **anchoring.** This means bringing gentle attention to a chosen object, and if attention wanders away, gently bringing it back. Think of anchoring as a ship dropping anchor in choppy seas. The ship stays close to the anchoring site despite the movement of wind and water. In the same way, when attention is anchored to a chosen object, it stays close to the object despite other mental activity. For the object of meditation, you may choose any object that affords the mind some measure of attentional stability. The standard meditation object (and my personal favorite) is the breath, but you can also choose the body or any sensory experiences such as sights, sounds, touch, or internal body sensations, or even the entire sensory field all at once as a single large object. One person I know found the sensation on the soles of his feet to be his favorite meditation object. That guy is obviously very grounded. And, yeah, I think his idea has legs.

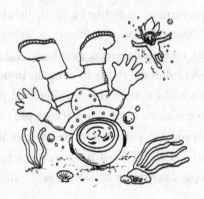

If anchoring is too hard for you, here is the second method: **resting.** Resting means exactly that, to cease work or movement in order to relax, that is all. When I'm physically tired after a hard workout, I sit down on my comfy chair and rest. Similarly, to rest the mind, all I do is sit down and allow my mind to relax. One way to rest the mind is to use an image. Imagine a butterfly resting gently on a flower moving slowly in the breeze. In the same way, the mind rests gently on the breath. Another way is to use this mantra, "There is nowhere to go and nothing to do for this one moment, except to rest." Resting is an instinct—we all know how to do it. The idea here is to turn resting from an instinct to a skill.

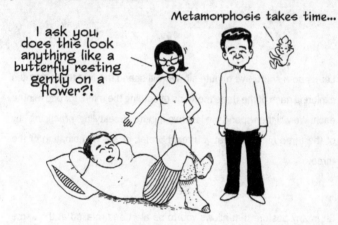

If resting is still too hard for you, here is the third method: **being.** Being means shifting from doing to being. It means not doing anything in particular, just sitting and experiencing the present moment. You can think of it as non-doing, or sitting without agenda, or simply just sitting. The key ingredient of this practice is being in the present moment. As long as your attention is in the present, you are doing it right. Alternatively, and slightly more poetically, you can think of the key ingredient as **knowing.** As long as you *know* you are sitting, you are doing it right.

All three practices above, and all practices that settle the mind in general, have two features in common: they all involve some degree of **mental stillness** and **attention to the present moment.** Because of that, they all lead to the basic meditative state, which is the state where the mind is **alert** and **relaxed** at the same time. When the mind is alert and relaxed, over time, it will calm down the same way the snowflakes in the snow globe settle down, and the mind abides in a state where it is both calm and clear.

Let us give it a try.

FORMAL PRACTICE: EXPLORING WAYS TO SETTLE THE MIND

Let us do a short, five-minute sit. We will spend the first three minutes exploring each of the three methods of settling the mind, for one minute each. We will then spend the last two minutes freestyling, practicing any of the three methods that you most prefer, or any combination of the three.

Setup

Sit in any posture that allows you to be alert and relaxed at the same time, whatever that means to you. You may keep your eyes opened or closed.

Anchoring (1 Minute)

For one minute, bring gentle attention to the breath, or the body, or any sensory object that affords the mind some measure of attentional stability. If attention wanders away, gently bring it back.

Resting (1 Minute)

For the next minute, rest the mind. If you like, you may imagine the mind resting on the breath the same way a butterfly rests gently on a flower. Or say to yourself, "There is nowhere to go and nothing to do for this one moment, except to rest."

Being (1 Minute)

For the next minute, shift from doing to being. Sitting without agenda. Just sit and experience the present moment, for the duration of one minute.

Freestyle (2 Minutes)

For the next two minutes, you may practice any one of the three methods above, whichever your favorite is, or you may switch between them at any time.

After doing one or a few rounds of the above exploration, it is useful to decide which method of settling the mind is your favorite. This will be your primary method for settling the mind. Don't worry about making a "wrong" choice—there is no wrong choice, plus you can change your mind anytime. It is sort of like choosing your favorite flavor of ice cream—there is no wrong choice, and you can change your mind anytime.

I recommend doing the exercise of settling the mind at least once a day, for at least one minute a day. Most teachers I know recommend twenty minutes a day, but you may do it for any duration you want, knowing that no duration is too long. Even seasoned meditators on formal retreats may choose to do this one very basic meditation for ten or more hours a day, so don't be shy about practicing settling the mind for as long as you want.

FORMAL PRACTICE: SETTLING THE MIND

Choose one of the three methods of settling the mind (anchoring, resting, or being) to be your favorite method. Sit in any posture that allows you to be alert and relaxed at the same time, whatever that means to you. You may open or close your eyes.

Settle your mind using your favorite method for any duration of time. You may switch between methods at any time.

Different Meditative Strokes for Different Meditating Folks

Why did I present three methods to settle the mind? Why not just one? Is it because I'm greedy? No, it is not (just) because I'm greedy. I did that because of a very important fact about meditative training that every meditation teacher and trainee needs to be keenly aware of, which is that each person has a slightly different mental disposition, and therefore, different training methods work better for different people.

Even among these three simple methods for training the most basic of meditative states, one method may work better for some people than others. One person might find anchoring difficult because he gets stressed out trying to anchor attention on the breath. Another person struggles with the being (non-doing) method because she keeps being bothered by the question, "Am I doing it right?" For her, anchoring might be more comfortable because she knows precisely when she is "doing it right." Another person might be attracted to the resting method because she plays a lot of sports so she knows precisely what it means to rest and she can as easily do it for the mind as she does for the body. Given that settling the mind is the most important of all meditative practices, I decided to suggest three different methods that cover a fairly wide spectrum of dispositions. In general, it is important for teachers and trainees not to be too attached to any one training method. In addition, in my opinion, it is imperative for a teacher to understand *how* a training method works, its pros and cons, and then be able to explain it to the trainee to help him find the optimal methods for himself.

It is also useful to note that even for the same person, the optimal meditation method may change according to the situation. For example, my own favorite method of settling the mind is anchoring to the breath, but on some days, having had a very exhausting day at work, I may decide the best practice is resting, not anchoring.

That leads us to an important practical question: how do we know what is the best practice at any given moment? Over time, with sufficient practice, you will develop an intuition. You'll become like a skillful sushi chef who can intuitively adjust for slight variations between one batch of rice and another to always prepare perfect sushi rice. In the same way, you can intuitively vary your practice to adjust for day-to-day variations in your state of mind. What if you haven't yet developed the intuition—what to do, what to do? No worries, all you need to do is experiment. First, you experiment to figure out your favorite method for settling the mind. Then, at every meditation session, start with your favorite method. If for any reason you feel the need to change the method, feel free to do so at any time, and after changing it, if you feel you want to come back to your favorite method, come back at any time. There is no downside to experimenting, and there is no way to do it wrong; it's a game rigged in your favor—if you play, you win. When in doubt, you can just stick to your favorite method and trust that it is fine. It's like a novice sushi chef who hasn't yet developed the skill to adjust for slight variations between different batches of rice. As long as he follows the standard recipe, he can still produce tasty sushi rice. His rice may not always be perfect like the master's, but it is still tasty.

In general, never be shy to experiment, and never be afraid to vary your practice from day to day. Of course, if you prefer to stay with the same practice for many years, don't be afraid to do that either. Nobody is going to call you names.

I Don't Settle the Mind—
The Mind Settles Itself

The snow globe analogy yields an important insight about what you can and cannot control. You have direct control of whether you shake the snow globe or settle it on the table, but you have no direct control over the state of the water and snowflakes in it. You cannot, for example, put your hand inside the snow globe to hold the water down and you cannot push down the snowflakes with your fingers. However, being wise to the laws of physics and all, you know that by settling the snow globe on the table and giving it time, the water will calm down and the snowflakes will settle by themselves. Therefore, if you desire calm and clear water in the snow globe, you know that you need to settle the snow globe on the table and then allow the laws of physics to do their thing.

It is similar with the mind. We really do not have direct control over whether the mind is settled or not, but what we can do is create the conditions conducive to the mind being settled and then allow the mind to take its own time to settle itself.

This is an important lesson you will learn over and over again in your meditative practice, that a vital key to practice is to put effort into creating the right conditions for what you want to happen, and then to let go and allow things to happen (or not happen) on their own. In this sense, meditation is like farming. A wise farmer creates all the conditions conducive for crops to grow—she prepares the ground, plants the seeds, and makes sure there is enough water, fertilizers, and sunlight, and then she thinks, "I have done all that I can. Now I allow nature to do what it does." This analogy is especially appropriate since the traditional Sanskrit word for meditation is *bhavana*, which literally means "cultivation." A key aspect of meditation is the skillful combination of **wise effort and letting go.**

I'm practicing bhavana with bananas!

The snow globe analogy has its limitations. It does not capture the important fact that the more often you practice, the more quickly and easily the mind settles, due to a feature of the mind called

familiarization. The more the mind is in contact with any mental quality (such as calm or joy), the more familiar it becomes with it, and the more familiar the mind becomes with that mental quality, the more quickly and easily it gets it. Familiarization is the other key aspect of meditation. Familiarization is so important in meditation that the Tibetan word for meditation literally means "to become familiar."

Even right here, working on the simplest and most basic of meditative skills, you see the importance of wise effort, letting go, and familiarization. These three qualities apply to all your training, from here right up to mastery. Know them well—they will be your constant guides on this journey.

Meditation Is Not About Not Thinking

One of the biggest misconceptions about meditation is that it involves "emptying your mind of all thoughts." This one misconception is more responsible for turning people away from meditation than any other that I know of. Many beginners mistakenly think that they are supposed to have no thoughts during meditation, and then when they find thought after thought after thought cascading endlessly and uncontrollably in the mind like a raging waterfall, they decide that meditation is impossible and they give up.

No, meditation is not about suppressing thoughts. Instead, meditation is about allowing the mind to settle on its own terms, in its own time, which includes allowing thoughts to arise as and when they want to. It is true that over time, with practice, as the mind becomes more deeply settled, the stream of thoughts slows down and eventually goes from being like a raging waterfall to being like a fast-flowing river, then more like a slow-flowing stream, and finally, the mind is like a placid lake. Over time (in my own case, after many, many hours of meditation practice), the mind learns to quiet down on demand, but that does not come from suppressing the process of thinking—instead, it comes from learning to give the mind the space and time to settle on its own terms. Meditation is not what you think, or not think.

Right now, I'm sort of at the Chinese Water Torture stage.

Mind Training Is Like Cooking: The Three Mental Factors in Meditation

When I was growing up, one of my neighbors was a nice lady whom I called Auntie Stella. Auntie Stella was, by far, the best cook in the neighborhood. I remember her fondly because after my mom started to learn to cook from her, she (Mom) became a great cook and I was a beneficiary. I remember one day when I was in my early teens, I asked Auntie Stella for the secret to being a great cook. I had my notepad ready anticipating an elaborate answer, but no, she just said, "It is very simple—it is all about the control of the fire." I was incredulous at first. Surely it can't be that simple, I protested. She illuminated me with numerous examples. She said, for example, there is a reason she used a clay pot rather than a metallic pot for a particular dish, which is because of the way clay pots distribute and retain heat. There is a reason one puts in the garlic, and then the meat, and then the vegetables in a stir-fry, and that is because each cooks best at a different temperature. The reason you cook rice in cold water, not hot water, is because if you put the rice in hot water, the outer layer of the rice becomes an insulating layer that prevents the inner layer from being cooked. I was fascinated. She was right, the secret to effective cooking is the skillful management of energy.

I relearned the same lesson years later when I took up meditation. The secret to effective meditating is the skillful management of effort. The Buddha offered a similar analogy, but because he didn't have the fortune of being Auntie Stella's neighbor, his analogy did not involve cooking. Instead it involved goldsmithing. The Buddha taught that a skillful goldsmith does three things while working on a piece of gold: periodically he strengthens the fire, periodically he sprinkles water onto the gold, and periodically he examines the gold closely. Similarly, a skillful meditator periodically does three things: periodically he arouses mental energy, periodically he calms the mind, and periodically he watches the

GOLDILOCKS & THE 3 BODHISATTVAS

mind with equanimity.[1] These three factors balance each other. If there is too much mental energy, the mind may be restless; if there is too much calmness, the mind may be dull; and if there is only equanimous watching without the other factors, there may be insufficient concentration to advance into deep wisdom.

Simply put, skillfully managing energy in meditation boils down to balancing three mental factors: **mental relaxation, mental energy, and equanimous watching.** On a day-to-day basis, we need all three at once, always together, supporting and bringing the best out of each other, sort of like the Three Stooges. When somebody needs to act bossy, Moe steps up; when a fiddle needs to be played, it's Larry; and when you need a boxer in the ring to raise a thousand dollars for the orphanage, that's Curly. Each of the three stooges has his moment in the spotlight, but in reality, they are always the Three Stooges, always together supporting each other's roles.

Similarly, it is important not to neglect any of the three mental factors. But how? Turns out, it is easier done than said. The key is to practice equanimous watching, basically just watching yourself while you meditate. If you notice too much tension, then apply mental relaxation, and if you become sleepy, then apply mental energy. That is all. It is like the skillful goldsmith working on his gold, regularly watching his work, and he either strengthens the fire or sprinkles water as needed. **The key is watching.**

Puppy Dog Meditation

Here is a fun way to systematically practice all three mental factors— mental relaxation, mental energy, and equanimous watching—in the same sitting. Think of it as stretching your mental muscles. This meditation comes in five steps, each with its own story.

The first step is to **relax.** The story begins with you and your cute little puppy sitting under a tree, just relaxing, doing nothing in particular. Your puppy is young, energetic, and curious. She likes to wander around, but she also likes you, so she generally likes to stay close to you even while wandering. Every now and then, though, she wanders too far for your comfort, and when that happens, you gently and lovingly carry her back to the base of the tree. Awwwwww. So cute. The tree represents your breath, and the puppy represents your mind. In this step of the meditation, just relax and allow the mind to wander a little, and if it wanders too far away, just gently and lovingly carry it back. How far is too far? I think as long as the breath is in the background of attention, or you completely forget the breath but for no more than a few seconds at a time, it is good. Actually, it doesn't really matter, because the key practice at this step is mental relaxation, so as long as you are relaxed, all is fair game.

The second step is to **rejoice.** At this point in the story, the puppy has spent some time with you, her human. She has become familiar with you, she loves you, and she generally likes to sit next to you. When she does, you rejoice, having such a lovely being sitting next to you. She still likes to wander around—she is still a puppy after all—so she is not always sitting next to you, but even when she is running around, you still look at her and rejoice, "I'm so happy to have this puppy." Similarly, the mind at this time is a little more relaxed and a little more settled. Being settled, it is now easier to bring the mind to the breath. When you do, take the time to rejoice, thinking, "Mind is settled on the breath. I am happy." And even if the mind is wandering away, take the time to rejoice in having a breath before bringing it back.

The third step is to **resolve.** At this point in the story, the puppy has grown into a beautiful young dog and is now old enough for training. During training, you are gentle and loving, but at the same time, you are also a firm enforcer of discipline. You show a certain resolve. When you say, "Sit," you expect the dog to sit, and she will get no cookie and no positive reinforcement from you until she does so. Whatever order you give, you resolve for it to be obeyed, and you enforce discipline in a firm but gentle and loving way. In this way, you train the dog. Similarly, the mind at this time is a little more receptive to training, and you resolve to train it. Specifically, you resolve for your full attention to stay on the breath. Whenever attention wanders away from the breath, firmly but gently and lovingly bring attention back to the breath.

The fourth step is to **refine.** At this point in the story, your young dog is properly trained and it is time to refine her skills. She now obeys basic commands to sit, stand, and so on. Now you step beyond the basics to train her in a more demanding task, such as hunting for truffles. She develops the skills to know the truffles she is smelling for, find them in the ground, dig them out, and have the discipline not to eat them. Similarly, your attention at this time has gained some level of stability, and it is time to refine it a little. Specifically, the instruction is to "attend to the subtle nature of the breath," whatever those words mean to you.

The final step is **release.** At this point in the story, your dog is well trained. You unleash her, allow her to run around, trusting her to do whatever needs to be done and to come back on your call. Similarly, the mind at this time is relatively settled and refined, so let go of all effort and allow the mind to just be.

That is the practice. It covers all three mental factors of mental relaxation, mental energy, and equanimous watching. "Relax" and "rejoice" cover mental relaxation, "resolve" and "refine" cover mental energy, and "release" covers equanimous watching. As part of physical training, it is always good to do some stretching so that your muscles and tendons can cover their full dynamic range. I think of the Puppy Dog Meditation as the meditative equivalent of a stretching exercise. It is very healthy. I encourage doing this often.

FORMAL PRACTICE: PUPPY DOG MEDITATION

You can do the Puppy Dog Meditation for any length of time. In this exercise, let's spend two minutes in each of the five steps for a ten-minute exercise, but you are free to adjust the length of each step in any way.

Setup

Sit in any posture that allows you to be alert and relaxed at the same time, whatever that means to you. You may keep your eyes open or closed.

Relax (2 Minutes)

Relax and allow your puppy to wander, but if she gets too far away, gently and lovingly carry her back. In the same way, relax and allow the mind to wander. The key is to relax, but feel free to bring the mind back to the breath at any time.

Rejoice (2 Minutes)

Now, the puppy is familiar with you and loves you, and she likes to sit next to you. When she does, you rejoice. If you catch her wandering, also rejoice at having such a lovely puppy before gently bringing her back. In the same way, when you find the mind being settled on the breath, rejoice, thinking, "Mind is settled on the breath. I am happy." If the attention wanders away, rejoice, thinking, "I have a breath. I am happy." Then gently bring attention back to the breath.   *(continued)*

Resolve (2 Minutes)

Now the puppy is a young dog and is ready for training. During train-ing, you resolve to firmly enforce discipline, in a gentle and loving way. In the same way, you train the mind. Resolve for your full attention to stay on the breath. Whenever attention wanders away from the breath, firmly but gently and lovingly bring it back.

Refine (2 Minutes)

Now that your young dog is properly trained, it is time to refine her skills. In the same way, it is time to refine the training of the mind. For two minutes, attend to the subtle nature of the breath, whatever those words mean to you.

Release (2 minutes)

Your dog is well trained and can be unleashed. In the same way, the mind can be released. Let go of all effort and allow the mind to just be.

Oh, I didn't tell you the name of the dog, did I? Since she is a fe-male dog, I call her "Karma."

Depending on your cultural background, life circumstances, and mental disposition, relaxation may or may not be your first challenge. Whichever mental factor needs the most work tends to appear more prominent. My first meditation teacher, the late Godwin Samararatne, had a funny way of putting it. He came from Sri Lanka but taught all over the world. He said, "When I teach in America, I keep having to tell my students, 'Relax. Don't work so hard,' but when I teach in Sri Lanka, I keep having to tell my students, 'Don't relax. Work harder.'"

When I first started meditation, it was a big struggle for me, and ironically, the struggle was to learn not to struggle. I must really have been the worst meditator in the world because I had one big problem that nobody else had: during meditation, I could not breathe properly. Why? Because I was too intense. I was a stereotypical Asian overachiever with a fragile ego, so I always put a lot of pressure on myself in everything I did. When I was nineteen, I took a cartoon drawing class taught by an elderly Indian gentleman with exacting standards. After he saw the stiff look on my face during one of the drawing sessions, he told me, "Relax, young man, it's okay. It's only cartoons." An Asian teacher telling me to relax—that was how intense I was, all the time.

Relax, it's only cartoons... but make sure they're all good or you don't get paid.

I brought that same intensity to my meditation practice, and no, it did not go well. I was so stressed about doing meditation "right" that I even lost my ability to breathe properly. To solve that problem, following my modus operandi, I struggled even harder. Surprise, surprise, that did not work one bit. After months of daily struggles, I finally gave up. But fortunately for me, I gave up in a disciplined manner: I continued sitting as I had committed to doing—I just stopped trying to meditate, that was all. I decided I would sit on a chair and literally do nothing. It turned out that nothing was precisely what I needed to do. After just a few minutes of sitting and doing nothing, I became aware of feelings in my body, so I just sat there being aware of bodily sensations. Some minutes after that, I noticed myself breathing. And then I told myself, "Oh, so this is what it is like to know that you are breathing." Following that, I sat there and continued to simply know that I was breathing. I felt at ease. My attention stayed on the breath for a while, and suddenly, my entire body and mind was enveloped with a sense of gentle joy. It lasted for about thirty minutes. That was the first time I managed to "meditate." It was also my first experience of the joy of meditation. It was the joy arising from ease.

For many months after that, this gentle joy came and went when I sat. It took a long time before I developed the skill to stabilize it, and then to access it reliably. However, from that one experience, I learned *the* most important lesson in all of meditation practice: first and foremost, establish relaxation, and if relaxation breaks, reestablish relaxation.

Relaxation is the basic competency in meditation that enables all the others. Mind training without relaxation is like a tree without strong roots—it is not sustainable. The skillful trainee establishes relaxation first and then builds on top of it. When relaxing, one should apply as little effort as possible, for the obvious reason that effort has a tendency of breaking relaxation. If the mind is not relaxed, do whatever it takes, including going for a short walk, lying down, even allowing your mind to wander a little.

After I realized how important it was, I spent many hours practicing relaxation in meditation. In other words, I spent a lot of time sitting and doing nothing except knowing that I was breathing. After a while, relaxation became a skill for me. I got calmer, my health improved, I started responding better to stress, and I became less of a dick than I used to be.

Paradoxically, when I got quite good at relaxation, I became restless with it. Even though I was relaxed, I had two major problems at that point: my attention kept wandering away from my breath, a lot, and I kept falling asleep in meditation, a lot. In meditation parlance, I was lacking attentional stability. That lack of attentional stability was becoming increasingly annoying to me, so I set out to fix it. But how? Once again resorting to my old overachiever's MO, I applied discipline and effort, but with a twist from what I'd already learned: relaxation first. And the twist worked. I gave myself firm instructions such as, "I will attend to every single in-breath and out-breath, not losing attention to a single breath, for thirty minutes." There was only one rule, the relaxation rule: first and foremost, establish relaxation, and if relaxation breaks, reestablish relaxation. In other words, I would not let the effort stress me out. Anytime I felt stressed out, I would temporarily abandon effort and return to relaxation before reintroducing effort.

That worked. With increasing effort, my attentional stability started strengthening. And then I decided to try something naughty, something that every one of my teachers at that time had wisely told me not to do: as an experiment, I turned my meditation into a competitive game.

I'm an engineer—I like gamifying things. I was on a private retreat at the time, and I decided to compete meditatively with myself. I timed myself (with a stopwatch) to see how long I could go without dropping my attention from a single breath. Every time I lost one breath, I'd note the time, reset the stopwatch, and start again from zero. I would set my "best score" and then try to beat it.

Um, I'm really not sure *Meditation Meditation Meditation Revolution* is going to be a big hit...

"Madness," you may say, but as usual, my madness had a method behind it. I figured that the reason meditation teachers tell you never to have any goal in meditation, much less a competitive goal, is because doing so breaks relaxation, and breaking relaxation is counterproductive. However, I reasoned that in my case, I already had reliable access to joy arising from ease, and because my meditation was already permeated with that joy, I could apply a high degree of effort toward a competitive meditative goal without breaking relaxation. That was the theory I decided to test.

The result of that experiment was accelerated progress. In just eighty hours of practice during that retreat, my "best score" went from six minutes to thirty. In other words, I developed the ability to keep my attention on the breath for half an hour without losing attention to a single breath, and to do so without stressing out.

Looking back at that experience from the vantage point of a more mature practice, and also from talking to other teachers, I realized I had quite accidentally done the skillful thing. Mental training requires a skillful balance of disciplined effort and joyful relaxation, which means the more joyful relaxation you can already count on, the more disciplined effort you can commit, and the more of both you have, the faster you can establish attentional stability.

With this and the previous chapter, you have everything you need to start **easing into joy.** As you practice this skill, you will begin to experience the freedom of peace and joy that doesn't depend on stimulation of your senses or ego. Because inner peace and inner joy are independent of worldly circumstances, they are available to you anyplace and anytime. The skill of easing into joy is the first of the three skills that will enable you to access them anyplace and anytime, on demand. In the next chapter, we'll learn the second of these skills: **inclining the mind toward joy.**

Daily Practice for Mind Training with Ease

Putting it all together, the first step is to understand that meditation can be easy and that even a single meditative breath is beneficial. Recognize that there is joy even in the first breath. Do the One Mindful Breath practice often—make it a habit.

Next, understand that we do not settle the mind—the mind settles itself. All we do is create the conditions conducive for the mind to settle. This takes unnecessary burden off us because we are not responsible for whether the mind settles; we are simply responsible for creating the conditions. With that understanding, do longer sits.

Twenty minutes or more a day is optimum, but any length of daily practice is good, even just for the duration of a single breath (and if you don't believe me, ask Gopi). If you like, you can spend the whole time doing your favorite mind-settling exercise (anchoring, resting, or being). If you prefer, you can also do the Puppy Dog Meditation. When sitting for longer, understand the role of the three mental factors, mental relaxation, mental energy, and equanimous watching, and adjust accordingly.

Above all, be at ease and just enjoy.

CHAPTER FOUR

What, Me Happy?

Inclining the Mind Toward Joy

In the introduction, we talked about three steps to accessing joy: easing, inclining, and uplifting. Chapters 2 and 3 addressed easing into joy and resting the mind there.

In this chapter, we will learn to incline the mind toward joy.

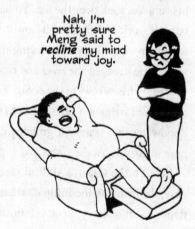

Nah, I'm pretty sure Meng said to *recline* my mind toward joy.

Flow the River

There is a beautiful description of mental inclination in some ancient texts. They compare it to mountain slopes. When the ground is sloped in a certain way, water flows effortlessly according to the direction of inclination. Similarly, when the mind is inclined in a certain way, thoughts and emotions happen effortlessly according to the nature of its inclination. If the mind is inclined toward joy, for example, then joyful thoughts and feelings tend to occur effortlessly.

This simple but critically important insight leads to an equally important practical implication, that the skillful way to train the mind is not to exert forceful control over the mind itself, but to change its inclination so that thoughts and emotions occur effortlessly in the direction one intends.

In Chinese history, during the reign of Emperor Shun (who lived sometime around 2200 BCE), what was then known as China was plagued by frequent destructive floods along the Yellow River. The emperor ordered a nobleman called Gun to solve the problem. Gun's strategy was to build a series of dikes and dams to block the flow of water. Given the technology available at the time and the massive scale of the problem, that strategy was probably bound to fail, and it did, spectacularly. After nine years of building dikes and dams, the strategy proved itself to be a dam-ed failure. After Gun passed away, his son, Yu, took over the job. Yu had had nine years to observe his father's work and figure out how it failed. As a result, Yu's strategy was the reverse. Instead of trying to stop the water, he would work with it. He dredged the river and cleared its bottlenecks to allow it to flow more freely toward the ocean. Even more skillfully, Yu also built a system of irrigation canals to turn some of the formerly destructive floodwater into water for growing crops. Yu is remembered in Chinese history as Yu the Great.

Like Yu the Great, a skillful meditator gains mastery of, in this case, the mind by inclining it rather than fighting with it. Inclining depends on one key faculty: familiarization. We noted earlier that

meditation *means* familiarization, in this case, to **familiarize the mind with joy.** The more the mind becomes familiar with joy, the more it perceives joy, inclines toward joy, and effortlessly creates the conditions conducive to joy. In English, the word *familiar* is closely related to the word *family*. In this sense, to familiarize the mind with joy is to turn joy into a close relative, a favorite member of the family, someone you can always rely on to be there for you. To become close with somebody, you welcome the person into your life and spend time with her, treat her with openness, pay careful attention to her, and get to know her well. Similarly, we will familiarize the mind with joy by welcoming it, staying open to it, spending time with it, paying careful attention to it, and getting to know it well. We'll spend the rest of this chapter getting to know joy. Hello, joy.

What, I Was Happy? I Didn't Notice

For the mind to get familiar with joy, first it has to notice it. So we train it to **perceive thin slices of joy.** In life, many moments of joy abound, but they are easy to miss because they are usually fleeting and not super intense. In other words, they come in thin slices both in time and in space. Once the mind is trained to see them, it can, and naturally will, incline toward them.

The training is simple. It is simply to notice joy. Whenever there is any joy arising in our field of experience, even if it is merely a subtle hint of joy, **simply notice that there is joy,** that is all. That is the entire practice.

Noticing joy is like noticing blue cars (or cars of any color of your choosing) on the road. When you're in traffic, blue cars pass you by all the time and, usually, you don't notice them at all. But if you play a game of noticing blue cars, you'll find that they are everywhere. There is joy to be found in many moments of our lives, though it may be subtle and fleeting. For example, with that pleasant feeling of warm water on the skin as we get into the shower, joy arises immediately, but we seldom notice it and it fades away in seconds. The practice is simply to notice when joy is there. The more you notice these thin slices of joy, the more they appear to be everywhere, because they have always been there. You just never noticed them before.

Noticing sounds trivial, but it is an important meditative practice in its own right. Why? Because noticing is the prerequisite of seeing. What we do not notice, we cannot see. And what we don't see, we can't understand. One of the ultimate goals of mind training is to completely understand four things: the nature of suffering, the causes of suffering, the nature of freedom from suffering, and causes of freedom from suffering. Complete understanding relies on clear seeing. Buddhist texts semi-cryptically refer to it as "seeing things as they are." Seeing things as they are begins with noticing things in the first place. Hence, the mere act of noticing becomes a meditation.

Let us begin by seeing if we can notice joy in a single breath.

FORMAL PRACTICE: NOTICING JOY IN ONE BREATH

Do the One Mindful Breath exercise from Chapter 2, which is simply to take one deep breath mindfully. If any hint of joy arises anytime during the exercise, **simply notice it,** that is all. If no hint of joy arises, no problem either; we simply **notice the absence** of joy.

By this time, knowing what you know about the habit loop (see Chapter 2), you can see how noticing joy could become a habit. Cue, routine, and reward: The cue is whenever there is any experience of joy, the routine is the simple act of noticing it, and merely being aware of joy is intrinsically rewarding. Hence, all three components required to form a habit are effortlessly present. All you have to do is notice joy. Do this for some number of exposures (maybe thirty) and a habit will begin to form. It's so simple, even Simple Simon can do it.

> ## INFORMAL PRACTICE:
> ## NOTICING JOY IN DAILY LIFE
>
> Whenever there is any experience of joy,
> just notice it. That is all.

Attending to Joy

Once you begin to notice joy, the next step is to attend to joy. What is the difference? The difference is in the level of care. Imagine there is a sick child in your house. To notice the sick child is to simply know that there is a child and he is sick, that is all. That may or may not lead to further actions, but the act of noticing stops right there, at merely acquiring knowledge. Attending is different. To attend to a sick child means you take direct responsibility for his care and nurture. You feed him, you help him relieve his pain, you nurse him back to health, and so on. To attend takes you out of mere data acquisition into nurturing responsibility.

In the same way, noticing joy is very useful, but even more useful is attending to the joy. To often notice joy begins to familiarize the mind with joy. To attend to joy is to go one step further, which is to consolidate joy in the mind. The way to do that is with intensity of attention. All you need to do is to pay intense attention to joy, that is all.

One reason I like the English word *attend* is because it suggests both directed awareness (as in "paying attention") and nurturing responsibility (as in "doctor attending a patient"). In attending to joy, both senses of the word *attend* come into play.

Joy on Demand

Let's try a short experiment. I'd like you to take three breaths. In the first breath, bring full attention to the process of breathing. In the second breath, calm the body. In the third breath, bring up joy. Give it a try now.

Were you able to bring up joy for the third breath? Some percentage of you reading this will be able to do it, because the first two breaths still the mind and calm the body, respectively, causing the joy of ease to arise. Those of you who have acquired the skill of seeing that joy will be able to hold it and amplify it. For those of you who are unable to do that, no need to fret—there is a very simple tool that'll allow you to cause joy to arise. That simple tool is: smiling.

Our facial expressions reflect our emotional state. It turns out, however, that the causation flows both ways. Facial expressions reflect emotional states, and they can also affect emotional states. One person to discover this is the eminent psychologist Paul Ekman. Paul is a pioneer in the study of emotions and their relation to facial expressions. One of his main contributions is the discovery of how emotions are encoded in facial muscles. Through years of careful study, Paul knows precisely which facial muscles are involved for every emotion. Paul also trained himself to manipulate those muscles in his own face in order to demonstrate the expression for any emotion. In the process, he and his associate noticed that when they were working on expressions of anger and distress all day, they felt terrible at the end of the day. Then they started measuring their bodies while they were making faces, and they discovered that their facial expressions alone were sufficient to create marked changes in the autonomic nervous system. For example, when Paul created the facial expression for anger, he raised his heart rate by ten to twelve beats, and his hands got hot.[1]

Given this insight, we can effectively invite joy just by smiling a genuine smile. Smile as if you are really happy. When you do this, you may create changes in the autonomic nervous system relating to happiness, and from these changes, you may experience joy. This works for me almost every time. It doesn't even need to be a full smile—a half smile works as well.

Let us make this into a short formal practice, starting with three breaths. In the first two breaths, bring full attention to the breath and calm the body. In the third breath, bring up joy. If necessary, bring up a smile or a half smile, whatever the words *half smile* mean to you. If there is any joy arising, attend to the joy by bringing full attention to it. If you like, you may rinse and repeat.

FORMAL PRACTICE: INVITING AND ATTENDING TO JOY

Sit in any posture that allows you to be alert and relaxed at the same time, whatever that means to you. You may keep your eyes open or closed.

Let us take three breaths. In the first breath, bring gentle but intense attention to the process of breathing. In the second breath, calm the body. In the third breath, bring up joy. If necessary, bring up a smile or a half smile, whatever the words *half smile* mean to you. If any joy arises, bring full attention to it. If you like, repeat this three-breaths practice a few more times.

When I take slow, deep breaths, I breathe at a rate of roughly six breaths a minute, so this practice takes me only thirty seconds. You can easily extend the three-breaths practice to three minutes by attending to the breath for one minute, followed by calming the body for the next minute, and bringing up joy and attending to it in the final minute. Or, if you like, you may play with the parameters in any way—there is really no harm in experimenting.

With this practice, the mind gets familiar with joy. With this practice, you can begin to develop the ability to **bring about joy on demand** in most ordinary circumstances. Why is this simple practice so powerful? Because it contains three elements conducive to joy all in one place: stillness of mind (from the first breath), ease and relaxation (from the second breath), and invitation and awareness of joy (from the third breath). Each of these is highly conducive to inner joy by itself. When combined, and when the mind is familiar with the combination, it gets very powerful. The only mental factors I know of that are more conducive to joy are loving-kindness and compassion, which we will discuss in detail in the next chapter.

The Joyful Mind Rocks at Meditation

One of the most important things I have ever learned is the central role joy plays in meditation. This understanding set me firmly on the path of joy in my meditation training and in my life. In the ancient texts of Early Buddhism, which is the tradition of my own meditation training, joy is very frequently mentioned. One particularly important text, *The Discourse on Proximate Causes* (*the Upanisa Sutta*), states emphatically that "the proximate cause of concentration is joy."[2] In other words, joy is the condition most immediately responsible for (meditative) concentration.

"The proximate cause of concentration is joy." There are three important nuances in this statement, one in its translation, one in its context, and one in its implicit assumption. The nuance in translation comes from the word translated as "concentration." In Pali, the original language of the quoted text, the word is *samadhi*. *Samadhi* is usually translated as "concentration," sometimes as "serenity" or "stillness." Unfortunately, all three translations are inadequate because each one captures only a partial meaning of samadhi. Samadhi is all three. Samadhi is a state of mind that is calm, serene, and relaxed, and one-pointedly concentrated, meaning attention is perfectly stable and still. Samadhi is extremely important in meditation—the ability to abide in it is one of the hallmarks of a highly accomplished meditator. I think the best translation of *samadhi* is "collectedness," based on its literal meaning of "to put together," or "to collect." The reason I'm mentioning this is to point out that joy is so useful in meditation, it leads all the way to some of the highest meditative states.

The second nuance relates to the happy fact that there is more than one kind of joy. The Proximate Causes text actually refers to three different types of joy in mind training, not one. The three types of joy, in their original Pali words, are *pamojja, piti,* and *sukha.* *Pamojja* is often translated to "gladness" and is described as the kind of excitement that comes from finding something that you like, something that you feel well-disposed to, in this case, the gladness in finding the teachings and seeing them benefit your life. In a sense, pamojja is the gladness relating to hope. *Piti* is often translated to "rapture," sometimes to "uplifting joy" or "energetic joy," and it is the rapturous joy that elevates the mind. *Sukha* is often translated to "happiness," sometimes to "bliss," "contentment," "pleasure," "non-energetic joy," or "gentle joy," and it is the type of quiet, sustainable joy that leaves you content. When used in a day-to-day context, outside of meditation, sukha also means general happiness, which sometimes confuses the sukha out of people reading the ancient texts. The proximate cause of collectedness is sukha, but pamojja and piti play important roles that lead to it. The reason I'm describing this nuance is to point out the fact that meditative joy is fascinatingly multifaceted and flavorful.

The third nuance comes from an assumption not specific to this particular text but sprinkled widely across texts in Early Buddhism: the idea of "wholesome" sources of joy. Wholesome means something that is conducive to the well-being of self and others, in the present and in the future. The Pali word that is translated to "wholesome" is *kusala,* also often translated as "skillful," which I find to be a skillful translation (making it meta-skillful, I think). *Kusala* is sometimes translated as "profitable," and I promise you this translation was not sponsored by Wall Street. A grossly oversimplified definition of *wholesome* that doesn't do it a lot of justice, but is sufficient for the purpose of this book, is this: a wholesome source of joy is one that is not contaminated with greed, ill will, or the seeds of future suffering. Kindness is a wholesome source of joy, for example, while joy derived from cruelty is unwholesome. Joy from wholesome sources is most conducive to collectedness of mind. Joy from an unwholesome source leads the mind away from peace, contentment, and collectedness, making it counterproductive, at least for the purpose of meditation. So remember to only use an uncontaminated source full of wholesome goodness.

You don't have to read the ancient texts to get the timeless points: there are different flavors of joy; there are different sources of joy, not all created equal; and the ability to remain calm, cool, and collected has a lot to do with joy, specifically joy from the right sources. In meditative terms, a joyful mind is highly conducive to meditation, and a meditative mind is highly conducive to joy. Once you start the cycle running, they reinforce each other and lead you into a deeper practice and a more joyful life. Hence, do not be afraid to use joy as a vehicle for your meditation, and do not be afraid to use meditation as a vehicle for a joyful life. You will profit in both places, in a wholesome, skillful way.

Attending to Joy in Real Life

Complementing the formal practice of inviting joy in sitting meditation are the informal practices of attending to joy in real life. Yay!

There are three sources of wholesome joy in daily activities that we can tap. One source is the type of behavior that uplifts the spirits, such as behavior involving generosity, loving-kindness, and compassion. These get a whole chapter to themselves, the next chapter.

Ethical behavior is another day-to-day source of wholesome joy. "Doing the right thing" contributes incrementally to a clear conscience, and from a clear conscience arises a joy that is very easy to miss called the **joy of blamelessness.** In ancient texts, cultivating the joy of blamelessness is compared to a farmer clearing the ground by removing weeds and stones before he plants his crops. By clearing the ground, his crops will grow better. In the same way, the joy of blamelessness clears the mind of some significant percentage of shame, guilt, worry, and regret, thereby affording the mind the ease that is highly conducive for meditation. In turn, attending to the joy of blamelessness gives the mind positive reinforcement for ethical behavior, thereby making such behavior more likely in the future. Every time you make an ethical decision or engage in any ethical behavior, I encourage you to take a moment to think to yourself, "I have done an ethical thing. My conscience is clear. I am happy." If joy arises, bring full attention to that joy for at least one moment. This is the joy of blamelessness.

INFORMAL PRACTICE: ATTENDING TO THE JOY OF BLAMELESSNESS

When you make an ethical decision or engage in any ethical behavior, take a moment (in the present, or a little later) to think to yourself, "I have done an ethical thing. My conscience is clear. I am happy." If joy arises, bring full attention to that joy for at least one moment.

Another source of wholesome joy is attending to pleasant experiences in your normal, everyday activities. The practice is simple: when you do something that involves a pleasant experience, take at least one moment to attend fully to the joy that pleasantness invokes. That is all. For example, at lunch, bring full attention to the enjoyment of the first bite. The first bite is when you are most hungry, so it is also the most delicious bite. There is a thin but very satisfying slice of joy in there—don't miss it. Attend fully to that joy. This practice only asks that you attend fully for one bite, so if you're having lunch with someone, it does not take you away from your conversation. I mentioned another example before: when you first get into the shower, attend to the joy of the moment the water touches your skin. When you're with someone you love, take one moment to attend fully to the joy of his or her presence. There are many opportunities to practice attending to the **joy of pleasant experiences** throughout the day. At the minimum, if you eat, there are at least as many opportunities to practice attending to pleasant sensory experiences as there are the number of times you eat, so at minimum, many people can practice this at least once a day. If you are reading this book, chances are you belong to the population who get to eat at least once a day.

INFORMAL PRACTICE: ATTENDING TO THE JOY OF PLEASANT DAILY EXPERIENCES

Whenever you engage in an activity that involves a pleasant experience, take at least one moment to attend fully to the joy that pleasantness invokes. Some examples:

At each meal, attend fully to the enjoyment of at least the first bite.

When seeing a loved one, especially a beloved child, take one moment to appreciate that he or she is there, and attend fully to that joy.

When holding hands with a loved one, take one moment to attend fully to the joy of that contact.   *(continued)*

When taking a shower, attend fully to at least one moment of the enjoyment of the body's contact with water.

When relieving yourself in the toilet, attend fully to at least one moment of the pleasure of relief.

When out on a nice day, take one moment to attend fully to the enjoyment of the weather.

When walking, take one moment to attend fully to the joy of being able to walk.

In general, when seeing, hearing, smelling, tasting, or touching something pleasant, bring full attention to the joy for at least one moment, and when interacting with a beloved person, bring full attention to the joy of being with that person for at least one moment.

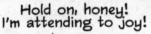

This one, simple, almost trivial practice has many very compelling benefits. The first compelling benefit is that relationships become more fulfilling. For many of us, we do not fully value people we love until we are separated from them. For example, it's only after your kids go off to college that you wish to yourself that you had paid more attention to them while you still had them. This practice preempts a lot of that regret by giving you many moments of joy in fully valuing their presence while they are still here. Every time you pay a moment of full attention to the joy of a loved one's presence, you value them a little more, you enjoy them a little more, you are happier, and the relationship becomes stronger.

The next compelling benefit is a significant increase in happiness. Many of us have so many joyful moments that we totally miss because we're not paying attention to them. With this practice, we don't just notice them—we revel in them by giving them at least one moment of full attention. Joy increases, but more important, it leads to something else: **gratefulness.** Very soon, as you begin to fully enjoy all these little pleasures in life, you take them less and less for granted. You become more and more grateful. A lot of research has shown gratefulness to be an important cause of overall happiness in life.[3] Regularly noting things you are grateful for in a gratitude journal can significantly increase happiness.[4] My friend Shawn Achor, author of *The Happiness Advantage,* suggests that spending two minutes a day scanning the world for three new things you're grateful for, and doing that for a mere twenty-one days, is the fastest way to learn optimism.[5] Shawn also suggests a nice daily practice he calls the "doubler," which is to recall one positive experience of the day in detail, because the brain can't tell the difference between visualization and actual experience, so by doing this, you double the experience.

Keeping a gratitude journal, finding new things to be grateful for, and recalling a joyful experience every day are all great ideas. However, taking one moment to fully attend to every joyful experience has the advantage of taking no time and no effort. You can do it many times a day, in real time, with zero delay in gratification.

This practice also benefits meditation practice in at least two ways. First, every moment of paying full attention to joy amplifies attention a little more, and since attention training lies at the core of meditation, that moment of paying full attention to joy is in fact a moment of meditation practice, and over time, it adds up. Second, and more important, this joy that you cultivate in ordinary activities makes the mind more attuned to joy during sitting meditation. Sometimes as I sit, the mind suddenly notices, "Oh look, this breath is so pleasant, I'm so happy." Out of nowhere, I get a bonus jolt of piti and sukha (energetic joy and gentle joy) to fuel my meditation. The more you incline your mind toward joy in real life, the more joyful and productive your meditations will tend to be.

"Someday, I Will Die," and Other Happy Thoughts

One of the biggest hindrances, possibly *the* biggest hindrance, to perceiving the very many moments of joy in daily life is a phenomenon called **habituation,** which for our purpose simply means we take things for granted. Imagine getting the promotion you always wanted. Initially, you'll experience euphoria, but after a few days or weeks or months, your emotional reaction to your promotion can be summarized in one very descriptive word I learned from teenagers: *meh*. Same thing with getting your dream car, or dream house, or dream job, or dream anything else. After some time, meh.

My attitude to life in general is just, "Meh".

There are three ways to overcome habituation, two of which we have already discussed. The first way is by deploying attention, for example, by attending to joy. In theory, it is possible to completely overcome habituation with the mastery of attention. One of the early scientific studies on Zen monks looked at this phenomenon way back in 1966.[6] The study measured people's neurological reaction to a repeated click stimulus at regular intervals while they meditated. A novice meditator's brain, unsurprisingly, habituates to the sound and after just a short while stops reacting to that sound. In contrast, a master meditator can choose to not habituate to the sound. So even after many clicks, the highly trained mind is still reacting to each click almost as if hearing it for the first time. Zen tradition poetically refers to this as "Zen mind, beginner's mind." Even for those of you reading this book who are not Zen masters (you know who you are), the more you practice mindfulness, the more likely you will be able to down-regulate habituation on the strength of your mindfulness and enjoy the pleasures of the day anew.

The second way to overcome habituation is with gratefulness. Gratefulness brings into proper perspective how precious each joyful experience actually is. Some examples: That promotion I got is so precious—I know because I worked years for it. Owning my car and my house are both precious, and I know because I saved up for years for my house and my car. Having a child who loves me is so precious—I know many people who do not. Having good health is so precious. Having a good livelihood is so precious. Living in a peaceful country (i.e., not in the middle of a war zone) is so precious. Having ready access to food and clean water is so precious. Being able to see the blue sky and green grass is so precious. In fact, everything pleasant in life is precious, because anything good can disappear with very little warning. I can lose my health; I can get laid off from my job; I can go blind in an accident; war can happen; civilization can collapse. Gratefulness helps us see that everything is precious, and the more you can see how precious things are, the less you will take them for granted.

The third and, possibly, the most powerful way to overcome habituation is with a strong awareness of mortality. Someday, I will die. Every single person I love will die, some of them before I do. Even if science and technology can extend the human lifespan to one thousand years, or ten thousand years, or even ten million years, eventually, I will die, and everybody I love will die. Awareness of death is one of my main daily practices; every day, at least once a day, I remind myself that I will die and everybody I love will die. Being aware of mortality changes everything. At the very least, it puts things into proper perspective, it gives us clarity into what is really important versus what is not so important, and it therefore changes how we prioritize things in our lives. My friend Ehon, for example, witnessed his best friend, who was the same age as he was, suddenly die in his twenties. That shocked him into realizing how short, precious, and fragile life is. It changed Ehon's direction in life and turned him into the successful young entrepreneur he is today. Steve Jobs, in his moving Stanford commencement speech in 2005, which he delivered after learning that his own death was imminent, said:

> Remembering that I'll be dead soon is the most important
> tool I've ever encountered to help me make the big choices in
> life. Because almost everything—all external expectations,
> all pride, all fear of embarrassment or failure—these things
> just fall away in the face of death, leaving only what is truly
> important. Remembering that you are going to die is the best
> way I know to avoid the trap of thinking you have something
> to lose. You are already naked. There is no reason not to
> follow your heart.

It's surprising that such a morbid subject is linked to happiness. One study shows that the less time someone feels she has remaining on this earth, the more likely she is to derive happiness from ordinary experiences, and therefore, the happier she is.[7] One BBC story titled "Bhutan's Dark Secret to Happiness" suggests that people in Bhutan are so happy because they think about death five times a day.[8] It also quotes a 2007 study that shows that subjects instructed to contemplate their own death are more likely to construct happy words such as *joy* when asked to complete stem words such as *jo_*.[9] So it is entirely possible that a keen awareness of one's own mortality is one of the secrets of happiness.

My daily awareness of mortality has one other wonderful outcome: it makes it very hard to stay angry at a loved one for very long. I think, "How would I feel if this person died tomorrow?" Well, I would be very sad, and I would wish I had been nicer to her while she was alive. With that thought, it's very hard to stay very angry for very long.

My recommendation to all of you: at least once a day, remember that someday, you will die, and that everybody you love will die. If for no other reason, than because it is true.

INFORMAL PRACTICE: AWARENESS OF MORTALITY

At least once a day, either in the morning shortly after waking up or in the evening shortly before sleep, or anytime in the day, remind yourself of these two things:

- Someday, I will die. I will die. Every moment I have is precious.
- Someday, every single person I love dearly will die. They will all die. Every moment I have with them is precious.

The Joy of Not Being in Pain

To not be in pain is one of the greatest joys in life. Once, I had a terrible toothache. I had a wisdom tooth that was growing sideways that broke into the molar in front of it, and I was in great pain. I needed painful surgery to remove that wisdom tooth, and I was in pain for days after that. I also had to repair the molar with a filling on the side, which eventually broke and sunk into the flesh on my gums, and I was in great pain. I had to have emergency dental surgery to fix that problem. The dentist gave me a root canal, but the tooth eventually broke anyway, and I had to have another surgery to fix that problem, which caused great pain. At every step of that process, I thought, "If I didn't have this pain, I would be *so* happy!" And a few days after the pain went away, I forgot to be happy, until the next time I suffered similar pain again, at which point I told myself again that if I didn't have *this* pain, I would be so happy, and once again, I forgot to be happy a few days after that new pain went away.

If I never forget to be happy that I am not suffering the pain of a toothache, I would always be experiencing the **joy of not being in pain.** Is there a way to do this? I realized the answer is yes, and it begins with inclining the mind toward joy.

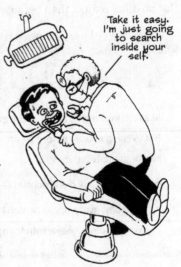

Take it easy. I'm just going to search inside your self.

My own discovery of the joy of not being in pain began slowly and gradually. I was doing the practices from this chapter, inclining the mind toward joy by paying full attention to the joy of my food, taking walks in nice weather, noticing sunsets, and all that. I wasn't really doing anything special beyond attending to joy. Over time, I realized that the number of items in my category of experiences that qualified as "pleasant" kept increasing. Experiences that used to be neutral (neither pleasant nor unpleasant) kept finding themselves moved into the "pleasant" category. Why? Simply because the more I paid attention to joy in simple experiences in life, the less I took them for granted, and the more I appreciated previously "neutral" experiences, the more they then appeared pleasant.

Then one day, I reached a tipping point. As I was drinking a glass of water in my kitchen, a powerful thought suddenly arose in my mind and refused to go away. The thought was: **"At this moment, right here, right now, I am not in pain."** Specifically, at that moment, I realized I was temporarily free from physical pain. I was not having a toothache, for example. Suddenly, for once, I remembered to be happy to not have a toothache. And to not have back pain, or shoulder pain, or pain anywhere else. And I did not have any pain walking or sitting or lying down. More than that, I'd just had access to drinkable water, which means I was unafflicted by thirst. I was unafflicted by hunger and cold. More than that, in those particular few seconds, nothing particularly bad was happening in my life. I was unafflicted by the mental tortures of hatred, anger, jealousy, envy, betrayal, anguish, grief, fear, or sorrow. I was unafflicted by the mental agitation of greed, want, loss, worry, or restlessness. Dude, I was just getting water in the kitchen.

And then it became clear to me, the greatest freedom that I enjoy, and also the one I take completely for granted and have barely noticed my entire life, is my temporary freedom from pain. I know that I am subject to old age, sickness, injury, trauma, betrayal, sorrow, fear, and death, so I know my freedom from physical and emotional pain is temporary, but still, right here, right now, I have that freedom. I spent my life thinking of freedom as the freedom *to* do stuff, but that freedom turns out to be trivial compared to the much greater freedom *from* affliction. I am free from most afflictions most minutes in the day, and I had not paid that freedom one iota of attention, nor rejoiced in it for one moment. Hence, if I can learn to abide in the joy of not being in pain, I will have plenty of joyful moments. Right there in my kitchen, I had stumbled on one of the greatest sources of joy in life.

One might ask, "Why doesn't it come naturally? Why aren't we all born to automatically always be joyful whenever we're not in pain?" I think there is a simple reason, which is that abiding in the joy of not being in pain requires us to notice the **absence** of pain, and noticing the absence of phenomena doesn't come naturally to us. When we are stimulated by the arising of a phenomenon—such as a sight or sound, for example—we sense it, perceive it, cognize it, and then thoughts arise out of it. In other words, the mind is stimulated to participate in that phenomenon. In contrast, the absence of a phenomenon produces no stimulus to lead to sensation, perception, or cognition. The only way the mind can participate is to volitionally bring awareness to the absence. We can listen to the sound of silence, for example. So it takes some volitional effort to become aware of the absence of something not happening, which is why it doesn't come naturally. The good news is, this awareness can be trained as a mental habit. The more you make a point of noticing the absence of certain phenomena, the less effort it takes, and the more you will do it automatically.

To train the mind to become aware of the absence of pain, from time to time simply check to see if you are in any pain, and where you are not in pain, just remind yourself of that, and if any joy arises from that thought, just attend to that joy. If you do not have a toothache right now, remind yourself, "I do not have a toothache right now," and attend to any joy that arises. Even if you are experiencing pain in one way, it is possible to remind yourself you are not experiencing pain in another way. For example, I may be having back pain, but not having a toothache, so I can still remind myself, "I do not have a toothache right now."

Even more powerful than noticing the absence of physical pain, you can notice the absence of mental and emotional pain. For example, if you are not experiencing any hatred right now, remind yourself, "I am not suffering the pain of hatred right now," and again, attend to any joy that arises from that thought.

He's read that Meng fella's new book.

INFORMAL PRACTICE: NOTICING THE ABSENCE OF PAIN

Periodically, perhaps once a day, perhaps more frequently, bring awareness to the body to see if there is any experience of pain. Do you have a headache, a toothache, neck pain, back pain, or a stomachache? If any of those parts of the body is not in pain, you may remind yourself, "I do not have a headache / toothache / neck pain, etc., right now." If any joy arises due to that thought, bring attention to that joy.

Periodically, perhaps once a day, perhaps more frequently, bring awareness to the mind to see if there is any experience of mental or emotional pain. Are you experiencing the pain of grief, sorrow, hatred, anger, jealousy, envy, want, grasping, fear, or desperation? If you are not experiencing any of those sources of pain right now, you may remind yourself, "I am not afflicted by the pain of grief / sorrow / hatred, etc., right now." If any joy arises due to that thought, bring attention to that joy.

Just Note Gone

There is a simple practice that can greatly enhance your ability to notice the absence of pain, though it isn't only concerned with pain. "Just Note Gone" is a powerful way of practicing with any phenomenon, whereby we train the mind to notice that something previously experienced is no more. For example, at the end of a breath, notice that the breath is over. Gone. As a sound fades away, notice when it is over. Gone. At the end of a thought, notice that the thought is over. Gone. At the end of an experience of emotion—joy, anger, sadness, or anything else—notice it is over. Gone.

This practice is, without a doubt, one of the most important meditation practices of all time. Meditation master Shinzen Young said that if he were allowed to teach only one focus technique and no other, it would be this one. Here are the instructions for the informal practice of Just Note Gone, from Shinzen's article "The Power of Gone."[10]

INFORMAL PRACTICE: JUST NOTE GONE

Whenever all *or part* of a sensory experience suddenly disappears, note that. By note I mean clearly acknowledge when you detect the transition point between all of it being present and at least some of it no longer being present.

If you wish, you can use a mental label to help you note. The label for any such sudden ending is "Gone."

If nothing vanishes for a while, that's fine. Just hang out until something does. If you start worrying about the fact that nothing is ending, note each time *that* thought ends. That's a "Gone." If you have a lot of mental sentences, you'll have a lot of mental periods—full stops, Gones!

And here are my suggested instructions for formal practice.

FORMAL PRACTICE:
JUST NOTE GONE

Sit in any posture that allows you to be alert and relaxed at the same time, whatever that means to you. You may keep your eyes open or closed.

Sit in meditation for as many minutes as you like. Apply intense attention to the end of every out breath, clearly seeing the moment it ends. At the end of an out breath, if you like, you may silently note to yourself, "Gone."

If any thought or sensation arises, see if you can watch it until it fades away. If it ceases at any time, even if for one moment, note its cessation. If you like, you may silently note to yourself, "Gone."

You may end this meditation at any time. At the moment the meditation ends, take note of its ending. If you like, you may silently note to yourself, "Gone."

The Just Note Gone practice changes the way we perceive phenomena in three important ways. First, it brings balance to our perception of sensory and mental events. Every sensory and mental event has three parts: arising, presence, and ceasing. Most of us are aware of arising and presence, but we are seldom aware of ceasing. In other words, our experience of sensory and mental events is unbalanced—we often see the coming but seldom the going. By noticing gone, you restore perceptual balance, thus moving toward seeing things as they really are.

Second, even more important than bringing balance to perception, Just Note Gone helps us clearly see impermanence in all

phenomena. In every experience of sight, sound, smell, taste, and touch, there is a moment of gone. Every sensory experience has a gone. Every sensual pleasure has a moment of gone. Even (or especially) the pleasure of sexual orgasm has a gone. By frequently seeing gone, the mind comes to understand the nature of impermanence. The mind realizes that, **"Whatever is subject to origination is all subject to cessation."** When the mind intimately understands the nature of impermanence, it begins to see the gratification of sense pleasures as an unsatisfactory way of creating lasting happiness. So it stops clinging so desperately to sense pleasure, and the less desperately it clings to sense pleasure, the less it suffers from being the slave of sense pleasure, the more freedom it enjoys, and the more joyful it becomes.

Third, and perhaps most important, is the ability to see that **self is a process, not an object.** We usually experience the self as an object, as if there is such a thing called a self. To a highly trained mind, though, things are a little more nuanced. When you can perceive mental processes in sufficiently high resolution, you may find that the mind continuously creates a sense of self in reaction to sense input and thoughts that arise. When the mind is so calm it does not react compulsively to sense input, nor does it generate any thoughts, there may be moments when the sense of self does not arise. When the mind is calm, sharp, and trained to clearly see gone, it may be able to see the moments when the sense of self has faded away, before the sense of self is re-created by the mind. It can then perceive the self as a continuously running process, not a solid object. Recognizing this, our sense of self becomes delightfully fluid and we gain a joyful sense of lightness in life.

Do Not Expect Every Moment, Meditation, or Day to Be Joyful

As you begin to incline the mind toward joy, your meditation sessions may become increasingly joyful. You may have more joyful moments in your day. I must warn you, though, to please not expect joy all the time. In general, the more you practice with joy, the more joy will occur and the more you will notice joy, but it is unrealistic to expect every meditation or every minute to feel good. Why?

The first reason is normal day-to-day variance in life conditions. Some days, you might be tired because you didn't get enough sleep, or your back might be hurting, or you suddenly remember a fight you had with your spouse three days ago that you're still fuming over, or you ate too much at dinner, or you're stressed from work. Some days you don't even know why you feel down. Even if you manage to bring up joy, there will be days when it fades away quickly and you're too tired to bring it back. So it is easier to bring up joy on some days and harder on others. In any case, even if the difficulty persists for days, please do not think that your training is failing. It is simply a reflection of imperfect mind in the day-to-day variance in an imperfect world. Even an accomplished runner may find on some days that she does not enjoy the run or cannot perform at her usual level. This doesn't mean her training isn't working; it just means she is having some bad or not-so-good days. In mind training, too, it is okay to have bad or not-so-good days.

Somehow I think your technique works better with puppy dogs.

The second reason is sometimes terrible things happen. Emotional pain naturally occurs then, even for experienced meditators who can access joy on demand in less extreme circumstances. The pain can last for months. Under such circumstances, it is important to continue formal and informal meditation practice, not despite it being hard, but precisely *because* it is hard. It is like physical therapy for a runner who gets severely injured when she is hit by a car. She may not be able to run for months, but this does not make her a failed athlete. Her painful struggles in rehab are not signs of weakness. On the contrary, her willingness to struggle shows spirit and strength.

I have gone through very painful periods when my practice was not yet strong enough to keep me from being overwhelmed by emotional pain. I beat myself up extra hard because I was an experienced meditator. I was *supposed* to be able to do this, but I was clearly failing—failing at bringing up joy most of all. "I must be more worthless shit than even I knew," I told myself. It unnecessarily added tons to my suffering. The example of the injured athlete helped me out of my painful rut. I want to caution everyone in training to be careful of this pitfall, especially on the path of joy. We will come back to this in Chapter 6, when we explore working with emotional pain.

On the other hand, you may be surprised. When you practice inclining the mind toward joy, joy tends to happen, even when you least expect it. When the slope of the mind—to use that beautiful metaphor again—tilts toward joy, it becomes that much more likely to happen. Chris, a student of meditation teacher Soryu Forall, observed that as a result of his practice, he started smiling "for no apparent reason":

> I am happier and more joyful than ever before.
>
> Here's how I know I am more joyful: I'm smiling more. In fact, that was one of the first indications to me that my meditation was going well. I used to think my progress would be marked by big, mind-blowing experiences. Instead I discovered something much subtler. Over time, something I refer to as the smile-reflex began to emerge. I would be sitting in meditation, physical pain would arise, and then I would smile, for no apparent reason. This began to happen off the cushion as well. I might find myself in some uncomfortable situation, maybe a little confused, nervous, or scared, and I would reflexively smile. Over time, as I practiced, it just became easier to smile, a real true smile. A true smile contains joy. And that started to bubble up more and more in my life. I used to be depressed, and I've always been socially anxious, but being able to truly smile and thereby access some joy, even if only for a moment, has been really empowering. When you're smiling there's not a lot of room for negativity, and people seem to notice. It's kind of

hard to explain, but I think I am happier and therefore less
negative, and people seem to be attracted to that. I recently
had a job interview, and despite being nervous, I was able to
smile and let some joy out. It seemed to work; I was offered
the job—the principal even told me, "I like you!"

Life is still hard—I still get swept away by stress and
fear, but I always rebound. Somehow I bounce back to this
happiness and the sense that everything is just perfect as it
is. As a result, I've grown the confidence to tackle whatever
issues present themselves. I realize there are difficult things I
need to do in this world, but I can't do them without an inner
happiness to rely on. Life is so serious that it necessitates joy
and fun. I hope that makes sense.[11]

Daily Practice to Incline
the Mind Toward Joy

First and foremost, notice joy. Cultivate the skill to perceive thin
slices of joy, both in formal meditation and also in daily life. You do
that by attending to joy. The more you attend to thin slices of joy, the
more easily you can access them.

The informal practices in this chapter can vastly improve your
quality of life without taking any time. For example, the practice of
attending to pleasant experiences in everyday details, such as bringing full attention to the first bite of each meal or the first moment
of every shower, is guaranteed to increase your happiness in life. In
addition, I highly recommend the formal three-breaths practice of
Inviting and Attending to Joy.

If you are a seasoned meditator, the Just Note Gone practice is especially important for you. It can greatly accelerate your meditative

growth. If you are not a seasoned meditator, you should probably focus on the easier practices, such as noticing joy in the breath, but still, I recommend practicing Just Note Gone from time to time.

If you do the practices in this chapter, you will soon incline your mind toward joy. Eventually, your mind will be so strongly inclined that joy becomes quite effortless, both in meditation and in life.

Losing My Mind, the
Happiest Day in Seven Years

CHAPTER FIVE

Uplift the Mind
in Seconds

The Joy of Heart Practices

Can you turn another potentially miserable day at work into your happiest day in seven years? Jane did it in just eighty seconds. We will see how she did it and how you can do it too.

So far, we have learned to ease the mind into joy and to incline the mind toward joy. In this chapter, we will learn the last of three steps in training the mind to access joy on demand. Here, we uplift the mind by giving it a healthy shot of wholesome joy, a cocktail of three sublime mental states: loving-kindness, compassion, and altruistic joy.

Loving-Kindness and the
Happiest Day in Seven Years

In many of my public talks, I guide a very simple ten-second exercise. I tell the audience members to each identify two human beings in the room and just think, "I wish for this person to be happy, and I wish for that person to be happy." That is it. I remind them to not do or say anything, just think—this is an entirely thinking exercise. The entire exercise is just ten seconds' worth of thinking.

Everybody emerges from this exercise smiling, happier than ten seconds before. This is the **joy of loving-kindness.** It turns out that being on the giving end of a kind thought is rewarding in and of itself. To simply *think* that I wish for one other person to be happy makes me happy. I suspect there is an evolutionary reason behind this. Humans are ultra-social animals. We survive as a species because we are capable of living and working closely together in large numbers. My friend the psychiatrist and author Tom Lewis, has a funny way of talking about ultra-sociality. He said he was at the local zoo looking at the tigers when a zoo employee told him they cannot

put two male tigers in the same space because they will kill each other. Tom suddenly realized there were ten thousand visitors in the zoo that day, and none of the five thousand human males were killing each other. That, he told me with an impish grin, is ultra-sociality. In order to have ultra-sociality, we must have the neurological mechanism for ultra-sociality to exist, and I think the ten-second exercise illuminates the underpinning of that mechanism: the joy of loving-kindness, that simply being on the giving end of a kind thought is intrinsically rewarding.

If that is true, we may have just discovered one of the most important secrets of happiness. All other things being equal, to increase your happiness, all you have to do is randomly wish for somebody else to be happy. That is all. It basically takes no time and no effort. This is another key life-changing insight in this book. You're welcome.

How far can you push this joy of loving-kindness? One time, I gave a public talk in a meditation center called Spirit Rock in California. As usual, I guided the audience in this ten-second exercise, and just for fun, I assigned them homework. I was speaking on a Monday evening, and the next day, Tuesday, was a workday, so I told the audience to do this exercise for Tuesday: Once an hour, every hour, randomly identify two people walking past your office and secretly wish for each of them to be happy. You don't have to do or say anything—just think, "I wish for this person to be happy." And since nobody knows what you're thinking, it's not embarrassing— you can do this exercise entirely in stealth. And after ten seconds of doing that, go back to work. That's all. On Wednesday morning that week, I received an email from a total stranger, Jane (not her real name). Jane told me, "I hate my job. I hate coming to work every single day. But I attended your talk on Monday, did the homework on Tuesday, and Tuesday was my happiest day in seven years."

Happiest day in seven years. And what did it take to achieve that? It took ten seconds of secretly wishing for two other people to be happy for eight repetitions, a total of eighty seconds of thinking. That, my friends, is the awesome power of loving-kindness.

Once I spoke to a class at Stanford University and assigned the same homework, to wish for two people to be happy once per hour during school hours. One of the students, Mischa, liked it so much, she called it her "happiness ray gun" and added a "pew, pew" sound effect in her head when she secretly wished for passersby to be happy. Please feel free to do the same.

INFORMAL PRACTICE: WISHING FOR RANDOM PEOPLE TO BE HAPPY

During working hours or school hours, randomly identify two people who walk past you or who are standing or sitting around you. Secretly wish for them to be happy. Just think to yourself, "I wish for this person to be happy, and I wish for that person to be happy." That is the entire practice. Don't do anything; don't say anything; just think. This is entirely a thinking exercise.

If you prefer, you can do this at any time of the day for any amount of time. You can also do it at any other place. If there is nobody present, you can bring someone to mind for the purpose of this exercise.

If you like, you may pretend you are firing a "happiness ray gun" at them and make "pew, pew" sound effects in your head. Batteries not required.

After you master the ray gun of joy, you may advance to the lightsaber of joy.

Familiarizing the Mind with the Joy of Loving-Kindness

There are many wonderful things about the joy of loving-kindness. First, it can be initiated with a single thought, and thoughts are easy to initiate. Compared to other sources of joy, for example, the joy from sensory pleasure requires access to a pleasant object that the mind hasn't already habituated to, which is not always easy to come by. Even the joy of ease, we learned in Chapters 2 and 3, requires you to put the mind into a state of ease, which requires some amount of practice for some people. In contrast, all it takes to initiate the joy of loving-kindness is a single thought, "I wish for this person to be happy." Every conscious human being I have ever known in my entire life knows how to initiate a thought. Hence, the joy of loving-kindness is highly accessible.

Second, this source of joy is very wholesome. In Chapter 4, we defined a wholesome source of joy as one that is not contaminated with greed, ill will, or the seeds of future suffering. Loving-kindness fits this definition to a tee, and more important, it is an antidote for ill will, giving it the extra wholesome goodness every mom approves of.

Third, like all other wholesome sources of joy mentioned in this book, the joy and the wholesome mental state it arises from reinforce each other, forming a virtuous cycle with each other. In this case, the joy of loving-kindness makes one more likely to feel kind and loving, which in turn makes one more likely to experience the joy of loving-kindness. Therefore, a key way to optimize the functioning of this virtuous cycle is to familiarize the mind with the joy of loving-kindness. The more the mind becomes familiar with that joy, the more clearly that joy is experienced, and the more strongly it creates the future conditions for loving-kindness. What is the best way to familiarize the mind with this joy? Yes, the answer is repeated attention. By attending to the joy of loving-kindness repeatedly, the mind becomes familiar with it.

Here is a short and powerful practice for familiarizing the mind with the joy of loving-kindness. We only have to do this for a small number of minutes. At the start of each minute, bring to mind someone you can very easily feel loving-kindness for. In general, the best person is someone for whom you have total unconditional love, such as your child. After you bring this person to mind, wish for him or her to be happy. The joy of loving-kindness will likely arise, and if that happens, bring full attention to the joy until it fades away. For the rest of the minute, just rest the mind. And when the next minute begins, start the cycle again.

FORMAL PRACTICE: ATTENDING TO THE JOY OF LOVING-KINDNESS

Sit in any posture that allows you to be alert and relaxed at the same time, whatever that means to you. You may keep your eyes open or closed.

Repeat this cycle once per minute: Bring to mind someone for whom you can very easily feel loving-kindness. Wish for him or her to be happy. The joy of loving-kindness may arise, and if that happens, bring full attention to the joy until it fades away. For the rest of the minute, just rest the mind.

When the next minute begins, start the cycle again, for a total of three minutes.

You can do this for however many minutes you choose. You don't have to stick to a once-per-minute regimen—feel free to rest your mind for as long as you want between each cycle. The timing is not important; the only thing that is important is attending to the joy of loving-kindness, that is all.

Loving-Kindness is the "Gateway Drug" to Compassion

Practicing loving-kindness leads to another very important quality that has the power to uplift the mind: compassion. What is the difference between loving-kindness and compassion? Simply stated,

loving-kindness is the wish for self or others to be happy, and compassion is the wish for self or others to be free from suffering. They sound like the same thing, but there are at least two major differences. First, compassion necessarily involves a motivational component, while that is not always true for loving-kindness. If you see somebody suffering, and if a strong feeling of compassion arises, you experience some degree of motivation to do something. That motivation, which may feel almost like a compulsion, is always present in the experience of compassion, to some degree or other. In contrast, that same motivation is not always present in loving-kindness. If you wish for somebody to be happy, and he isn't, sometimes you feel motivated to do something, but other times you just shrug and go like, "Eh, maybe he'll be happy tomorrow."

I had a conversation with the eminent psychologist Paul Ekman, in which he told me a story that brought home the compulsive nature of compassion. He told me of a study on heroes. There turns out to be at least two categories of heroes. One is the category of people who run into burning buildings, dive into rivers, or jump onto train tracks to save the lives of total strangers. Amazing human beings. Paul told me there is another, even more admirable category of heroes, which includes, for example, people living under Nazi rule who hid total strangers in their own houses to protect them. The first category of heroes made a split-second decision, not having a lot of time to think about consequences. In contrast, the second category had time to think about the dangers they were exposing themselves and their families to, and day after day, they made a conscious decision to continue hiding perfect strangers in their houses to protect them. So the second category of heroes is even more amazing than the first. The question is, why? Why would anybody risk their lives and limbs for total strangers, with no expectation of rewards? And why would anybody consciously do that day after day for months or years? Paul told me that when the heroes in both categories were interviewed, they all gave different variations of the same exact answer: I didn't have a choice. They would, for example, say, "I couldn't just let them die. What choice did I have?" Or they would say, "That kid was drowning, what else could I do? I couldn't just stand there and do nothing." In other words, all genuine heroism has one thing in common: the compulsion that arises from compassion. Loving-kindness seldom involves the same compulsion.

The second major difference between loving-kindness and compassion is that loving-kindness is easier for an untrained mind. To bring up loving-kindness, all one has to do is think, "I wish for this person to be happy." Following that thought, a warm and pleasant feeling is experienced in the area around the heart, and joy arises, which may or may not always be perceptible to the untrained mind, but in either case, the exercise is easy to do. In most cases, it leads to a few moments of delightful joy, but even in the worst case, nothing happens, there is no downside or difficulty. Compassion, in contrast, is significantly harder because it forces us to come face-to-face with suffering. To practice compassion, you need to think, "I wish for this person to be free from suffering." At the very least, it means you need to recognize suffering. Very often, you also need to perceive the suffering, feel the suffering, stare it right in the face. In the untrained mind, to stare suffering in its face, whether the suffering is one's own or others', often invokes fear, panic, aversion, or at the very least, great discomfort. Hence, the natural instinct is to look away.

When I was a novice meditator, I decided that compassion was too hard for me. "Hey, look, I'm no saint," I told myself. Looking at suffering is hard, too hard for a lowly mere mortal like me. There are many saintly, heroic people in the world who are much better human beings than I, so they can do that compassion thing, and I'll just sit here and chill, thank you very much. And yet, something kept nagging at me. Instinctively, I knew compassion needed to be a central part of my practice, but I didn't know why, and I was too chicken to find out.

What changed for me was reading about a scientific study conducted on a Frenchman called Matthieu Ricard. Matthieu was a young scientist who, after getting his PhD in cell genetics at the Pasteur Institute, decided he really wanted to dedicate his life to studying with great Tibetan spiritual masters and to practice Buddhism when he grew up. Forty years of monkhood and forty thousand hours of meditation practice later, Matthieu became one of the first meditators in the world with more than ten thousand hours of meditation training to have his brain studied with fMRI (functional magnetic resonance imaging, which measures brain activity by detecting associated changes in blood flow). It was the first time anybody was doing these studies with scientific rigor, so the researchers were not sure at all what would come out of it. They decided that they would study a few of the many meditation techniques, in particular the meditation on unconditional compassion, and they'd see what happened. When Matthieu was in the MRI machine meditating on compassion, and when he did the same with 256 electrodes on his scalp for an EEG study, the changes recorded by the equipment were so far off the charts that the researchers thought they were probably measuring some kind of artifact, so they had to recheck some of the equipment. But very similar results were obtained time and again with Matthieu and with many other long-term meditators, both monastic and lay practitioners, men and women, coming from the East or the West: the difference between these meditators and untrained subjects was not so much due to individual special qualities—although there were indeed some differences between subjects—but to the nature of the training they had gone through. All the meditators with more than ten thousand hours of meditation training were able to reproduce similar results in the same lab.

Besides not being a saint, I am also not a brain scientist. I read the charts and it wasn't clear to me how to understand them experientially, so I asked my dear friend, Richie Davidson, the lead investigator in these studies, to explain it to me in terms that even I can understand. Richie said to me, imagine the emotionality involved in seeing an elephant charging right at you, imagine instead having positive emotions of that intensity, and imagine being able to bring it up on demand, in a few seconds. That's what Matthieu's and other meditators' brains can do. Wow.

The most jaw-dropping thing about this experiment for me was Matthieu's recorded happiness level. In a measure of happiness in his brain, where zero is neutral and increasingly negative numbers denote the magnitude of happiness, -0.3 being described as "beatific," Matthieu's happiness is measured at -0.45.[1] The press nicknamed Matthieu the "happiest man in the world."

Huh. And here I thought I was the world's happiest man.

I was shocked. **Compassion is the happiest mental state ever measured in the history of neuroscience.** To me, I had always associated compassion with suffering, but the data just told a totally different story. Many great teachers in a large variety of spiritual and religious traditions over millennia have taught that compassion is a divine, joyful state of mind. I had always thought of the idea that compassion is a joyful state as an empty nicety typical of what spiritual teachers tell the civilians when they have to give speeches after meals. But no, the data shows that compassion is the most joyful state ever measured in the history of neuroscience. I later asked Matthieu in person and he confirmed that, in his own personal experience, there is nothing more joyful than compassion.

But how can this be? Isn't compassion all about seeing suffering? In fact, even the word *compassion,* from its Latin roots, means "co-suffering," or suffering together. How can a state of mind so deeply embedded in suffering possibly be associated with joy, much less the greatest joy? After I found the courage to actually practice compassion, I found the surprising answer: it is precisely the necessity of facing suffering that leads to the faculty for accessing great joy. How so? I realized that if I start by bringing the mind to a calm and stable state, and then let inner joy arise and permeate the mind, and in that state, I open myself to the experience of suffering, an overwhelming feeling of sadness will soon start to occupy the mind, leading to great discomfort in both body and mind. But if I maintain the calm and stable mind, and if the foundation of inner joy is so strong that it never completely disappears, I can experience sadness with equanimity.

When I experience sadness with equanimity, three qualities arise: courage, confidence, and most important, selfless love. Courage arises because when the mind sees suffering totally enveloping itself and still is able to stay equanimous, its fear of present-moment suffering weakens. With that courage, the mind has less fear of suffering in the future. Hence, confidence arises too. With courage and confidence, the mind sees all that suffering with clarity and fearlessness. When a mind that is clear and fearless meets suffering, it takes on the quality of a loving parent or grandparent tenderly cradling a sick child, wanting to see that suffering relieved. The sense of self-importance fades out, a feeling of interconnectedness fades in, and with that, selfless love is awakened. The Greek word for selfless love is *agape,* which some have described (correctly, in my opinion) as the highest level of love known to humanity, one that is committed to the well-being of others. I think this selfless love is the heart of compassion—it gives compassion its divine quality and yields profound joy.

I myself find it challenging to maintain this state. For me, I have to muster a fairly high level of inner peace and inner joy before it works, and it takes a lot of practice (perhaps thousands of hours) to be able to do that reliably and sustain it. However, even at my fairly immature level of practice, I can already feel its potency, and I can see why it can eventually lead to an unparalleled level of joy.

Once I was dining with Matthieu in a Parisian café. By this time, we had become good friends, but in reality, I see him much more as a master than a friend. Eager to learn from him, I wanted to test if my understanding of compassion practice was approximately right, so I asked him, "There is a lot of sadness in the experience of compassion, yet compassion is supposed to be a joyful state, so how is compassion simultaneously a sad and joyful state all at once?" Matthieu's answer confirms that my practice is on the right track, but he takes a slightly different approach to arrive at the same conclusion. He says it is important to understand there is a difference between healthy sadness and unhealthy sadness. He calls healthy sadness "the courage of compassion." He says this is the type of sadness that inspires a loving response in you that compels you to take courageous action to relieve suffering. The difference between healthy and unhealthy sadness is despair. **Healthy sadness is sadness without despair.** Sadness without despair comes from the confidence that you have the inner resources to deal with difficulties. Where do those inner resources come from? Training the mind.

Compassion is more potent than loving-kindness, but loving-kindness is much easier. More important, loving-kindness paves the way for compassion. If your wish for somebody to be happy becomes sufficiently strong, then you naturally also want that person to be free from suffering, so in that way, loving-kindness leads to compassion. Hence, the lazy way to cultivate compassion is simply to master loving-kindness. Just do a lot of loving-kindness practice, which is easy and joyful to do, and eventually, your loving-kindness will be so strong that every human being you see, your first instinct is to wish for that person to be happy. Ancient texts describe this state of mind like a vigorous trumpeter who can make himself (or herself) heard in all directions without difficulty. In the same way, the meditator's loving-kindness flows in all directions without difficulty. From that point, to move from loving-kindness to compassion, all you need is a little nudge to become keenly aware of suffering. The mind suffused with sufficiently strong loving-kindness, when keenly aware of suffering, always becomes compassionate. That is the easy, lazy path—and the reason I think of loving-kindness as the "gateway drug" to compassion. You start doing easy, gentle loving-kindness, and pretty soon, you'll end up doing hard-core compassion.

Or, as the renowned Indian Buddhist master Kamalashila is believed to have said, "If you temper your heart with loving-kindness, and prepare it like a fertile soil, and then plant the seed of compassion, it will greatly flourish."

A slightly more formal way of looking at the path toward compassion is this: compassion is not sustainable unless it is based on inner joy and equanimity. At a high level of skill, compassion can create its own inner joy and equanimity, setting off the mental equivalent of self-sustaining nuclear fusion. However, it takes a lot of practice to reach that level. Less experienced practitioners sustain compassion with the joy of loving-kindness, plus the joy and equanimity that come from inner peace. Inner peace comes from the ability to calm the mind on demand, which in turn comes from calmness meditation (see "One Mindful Breath," page 66, and "Settling the Mind," page 90).

Let us do a formal practice that paves this path from calmness to joy to loving-kindness to compassion. To me, the most important part of this practice is the joy of selfless love. If and when it arises, attend to it so as to familiarize the mind with it. The more the mind is familiar with it, the more it becomes a friend of the mind, the more often it wants to come visit and hang out.

FORMAL PRACTICE: CULTIVATING COMPASSION THROUGH PEACE, JOY, AND KINDNESS

Setup

Sit in any posture that allows you to be alert and relaxed at the same time, whatever that means to you. You may keep your eyes open or closed.

Settle the Mind (2–5 Minutes)

Settle the mind either with anchoring, resting, or being. You may anchor your attention to any sensory object such as the breath, or you may rest the mind on the breath like a butterfly resting gently on a flower, or you may simply sit without agenda. In any case, allow the mind to settle on its own.

Attend to Joy (2–5 Minutes)

If any joy arises, bring full attention to it. If necessary, bring up a full smile or a half smile, whatever the words *half smile* mean to you. If any joy arises, bring full attention to it.

Loving-Kindness (2–5 Minutes)

Bring to mind someone for whom you can very easily feel loving-kindness. Wish for him or her to be happy. The joy of loving-kindness may arise, and if that happens, bring full attention to that joy until it fades away. Repeat this cycle as many times as you like, resting for any amount of time in between.

Compassion (2–5 Minutes)

Bring to mind anybody who you know is experiencing suffering (who may be the same person as above). Bring attention to his or her pain. Sadness may arise, and it may even envelope your entire body and mind, causing discomfort.

If you are able to experience this sadness with equanimity, do so. If you cannot experience sadness with equanimity, you may simply sit with the sadness without equanimity. If that gets too uncomfortable for you, you may shift attention away from the experience of sadness to the sensations in the body. If even that is too uncomfortable for you, feel free to disengage from this sadness at any time.

Selfless Love (If Any)

If at any time during the compassion exercise, selfless love arises, bring full attention to it. This love is like the mind of a loving parent or grandparent tenderly cradling a sick child. This love is unconditional and divine. If any joy arises from this selfless love, bring full attention to it.

Closing (2 Minutes)

Let's end this session by settling the mind again for two minutes.

Thank you for your attention.

Rejoicing in All that (Juicy) Goodness

Loving-kindness leads to one other quality that uplifts the mind: altruistic joy. Altruistic joy is usually defined as joy derived from the
success and good fortune of others, but it can also refer in general
to joy that is free of selfishness, resentment, jealousy, and envy. It
is the direct opposite of the German word *schadenfreude,* which is
pleasure derived from the misfortunes of others.

Altruistic joy can be delicious because other people's good fortune
tends to be quite visible, so if only I'm capable of rejoicing at other
people's good fortune, I can rejoice a lot. For example, every year
in my company, there are two promotion cycles. Lots of people get
promoted, and usually, it's not me. Hence, if other people getting
promoted brings me joy, I'll be plenty joyful, I tell you.

The most surprising thing I have learned about altruistic joy is how
hard it is to cultivate. In my experience, altruistic joy is much harder
to cultivate than loving-kindness and compassion. Some meditation
masters appear to have arrived at the same conclusion. The revered
German-born Buddhist scholar-monk Nyanaponika Thera said, for
example, that "it is relatively easier for man to feel compassion or
[loving-kindness] in situations which demand them, than to cher-
ish a spontaneous feeling of shared joy, outside a narrow circle of
one's family and friends."[2] Why is that so? I'm not sure why, but even
among toddlers, compassion seems easier than altruistic joy. For example, when one toddler is crying, another will give her a hug to try
to make her feel better. In contrast, when one toddler is given candy,
another toddler doesn't go like, "Yay! *You* have candy, I'm so happy!"
The candy-less toddler is likely to cry out of envy or jealousy.

Having said all that, there is good news. There is a subset of altruistic joy that is easy and uplifting, and that is rejoicing in the inner

goodness and altruistic behavior of others. It is easy and uplifting because we are hardwired to be awed and inspired. Bring to mind somebody who you know is very kind and generous, and you feel awed, inspired, and uplifted. Rejoice! When you read of a woman who spends all her days volunteering at the local hospital to bring joy to cancer patients, you feel awed, inspired, and uplifted. Rejoice! When you hear of a man running into a burning building to save a total stranger, you feel awed, inspired, and uplifted. Rejoice!

One great feature of this aspect of altruistic joy is it can be applied even to oneself. You can rejoice at your own altruistic acts. Some people may think that any action that benefits self in any way (in addition to benefiting others) cannot be considered altruistic. In other words, self must necessarily be excluded from benefit in order for an act to be considered altruistic. I definitely disagree because, as a meditator, it is obvious to me that one's own mind is always the first beneficiary of any altruistic intention; therefore, it is impossible to commit any act out of true altruistic intent without first benefiting oneself. Take compassion for example. The Dalai Lama teaches, "Many people . . . assume that feeling compassion for others is only good for the others and not for oneself. This is . . . incorrect. Whether or not our kindness brings benefit to others will depend on a great many factors, some of which will be outside our control. But whether we succeed in bringing benefit to others or not, the first beneficiary of compassion is always oneself."[3] He even half-jokingly calls compassion being "wise selfish." I think it is important to be aware that all intentions of compassion and altruism necessarily benefit self (at the very least, they benefit one's mind). It is even more important to apply them skillfully to practice, and one way to apply them skillfully is to rejoice at one's own altruistic acts.

If you have taken time and effort to cultivate loving-kindness within yourself, or have made a generous donation to charity, or been kind to someone, or even saved somebody's life, rejoice! In the tradition of my own meditative training (Early Buddhism), it is considered wholesome joy to reflect on the good things we have done and to take delight in them. This is especially true in the case of generosity. In fact, in one lecture to laypeople, the Buddha went so far as to list out the worldly benefits of generosity, including being dear to people, being admired by good people, and gaining a good reputation.[4] What that says to me is that even the coarse, worldly benefits of my altruistic deeds accrued to me are worth reflecting on and rejoicing in, as long as I did the deeds with sincere intent of benefiting others.

Rejoicing in one's altruistic deeds is considered wholesome joy because it is joy uncontaminated with greed, ill will, or the seeds of future suffering. In addition to that, it provides three important benefits. First, it gives a reward signal to the mind and therefore inclines the mind toward goodness, making altruistic deeds more likely in the future. Second, it uplifts the mind. Third, it counters self-inadequacy and self-loathing.

I'm surprised by how widespread the problems of self-inadequacy and self-loathing appear to be. Actually, to tell you the truth, I myself suffer from a lifelong, persistent sense of inadequacy, constantly feeling that I'm not good enough. I have the appearance of many worldly successes in my life. However, being successful never took away my feeling of inadequacy—it only added to it. Why? Because at the height of every achievement, I'd look around and say, "Actually, I was just lucky that I was in the right place at the right time. I don't deserve this." I have a lot of problems owning my success because I know for a fact that only a small part of it is due to my own intelligence, hard work, and good-heartedness, while most of it is due to external conditions beyond my control that I had no role in creating. I don't own most of the conditions of my success, and therefore, I cannot own most of my success. There is, however, one thing I can and do fully own, which is the **intention** behind my actions. When I donate money out of an intention of generosity, I own that intention—that was me. When I sit in meditation with the intention of becoming a calmer, happier, kinder human being, I own that intention—that was me. Hence, one of the few things in my life that can reduce my constant sense of inadequacy is reflecting on my sincere, altruistic intentions, and by extension, the good deeds that result from the intentions and the occasional good outcome of those deeds (on those occasions when my good deeds go unpunished).

There was a period in my life when I was facing such great difficulties that my sense of inadequacy became acute. It got so bad that during my daily meditation, I kept being interrupted by this inner voice that told me, "You are a completely useless piece of shit." The worst part was I actually believed it. My mind was dominated by anguish, and I could not settle it. Then a wise teacher told me, "You know what your problem is? You do a lot of good for others, but you keep ignoring that fact. At the beginning of your next meditation, I want you to reflect on the good you have done for others." I followed the instructions. When I sat down to meditate that evening, I reflected on a few people who had told me that something I did for them brought them great joy and changed their lives. I reflected on my intention behind those deeds, and they were all intentions of generosity. Reflecting on those intentions and deeds inspired joy in me, and the mind was uplifted. Once it was uplifted, I regained my sense of humor and replied to the voice that told me I was a completely useless piece of shit, "No! I am *not* a completely useless piece of shit, only 95 percent useless." It was funny, and I laughed to myself inside. With uplifting joy thus established, the mind settled. The mind was still dominated by anguish, but it was also capable of settling, and because of that, it was able to experience the anguish with equanimity and with a firm foundation of joy that never completely disappeared. In doing so, compassion arose toward myself. Altruistic joy had, therefore, created the firm footing for equanimity and compassion to take hold.

I later found out that some teachers teach this as a skillful way to begin any meditation. At the beginning of every meditation session, uplift the mind with altruistic joy. There are two ways to do it. The first is by reflecting on your altruistic deeds and the pure intentions behind those deeds (as I described above). The second is by reflecting on the goodness or altruistic deeds of somebody you greatly admire and whom you aspire to become when you grow up (for myself, that person is the Buddha). With the mind uplifted by altruistic joy, all three meditative joys will begin to arise: pamojja (gladness), piti (energetic joy), and sukha (gentle joy). As we learned in Chapter 4, the proximate cause of meditative concentration are the meditative joys; therefore, altruistic joy at the beginning of sitting meditation is a skillful way of quickly getting into a settled meditative state.

Let us give it a try. We're just going to do a simple settling of the mind, but uplift the mind with altruistic joy at the beginning. See if that improves your experience in any way.

FORMAL PRACTICE: UPLIFTING AND SETTLING THE MIND WITH ALTRUISTIC JOY

Setup

Sit in any posture that allows you to be alert and relaxed at the same time, whatever that means to you. You may keep your eyes open or closed.

Uplift the Mind (2–5 Minutes)

Take a few minutes to:

Bring to mind one or more people to whom you have brought joy or benefit out of purely altruistic intent. Reflect on the deed(s). Reflect on the good intention(s) behind the deed(s). Take delight in your good intentions and deeds.

OR

Bring to mind somebody you greatly admire and whom you aspire to become. Reflect on the inner goodness or the altruistic deeds of this person. Take delight in the goodness of this person and his or her deeds.

Settle the Mind (5–10 Minutes)

Settle the mind either with anchoring, resting, or being. You may anchor your attention to any sensory object such as the breath, or you may rest the mind on the breath like a butterfly resting gently on a flower, or you may simply sit without agenda. In any case, allow the mind to settle on its own.   *(continued)*

Closing (1–2 Minutes)

Close by noticing if there is any joy present in the mind, and if so, attending to it for one or two minutes.

In addition to the formal practice, I also recommend the informal practice of taking a moment to rejoice in inner goodness and altruistic deeds whenever you see them.

INFORMAL PRACTICE: REJOICING IN INNER GOODNESS AND ALTRUISTIC DEEDS

Whenever you make a donation of time or labor, or do something out of altruistic intention, take a moment to think, "I am doing this out of altruistic intention. Having this intention makes me so happy."

Whenever you meet or bring to mind an admirable, inspiring person, take a moment to think, "There exists this wonderful person in this world. I'm so happy."

Whenever you see somebody performing an altruistic or heroic act, take a moment to think, "More good is being done in this world. I'm so happy."

So Much Goodness, So Little Time

The three qualities in this chapter, loving-kindness, compassion, and altruistic joy, are three in a collection of four beautiful qualities called *brahmavihara*. The fourth member of that club is equanimity, which is the mind that remains calm and free in the face of eight worldly conditions: gain and loss, honor and dishonor, praise and blame, and pleasure and pain. Equanimity, when applied to the other three brahmavihara states, also carries the flavor of impartiality, which means that loving-kindness, compassion, and altruistic joy apply to all beings equally. I almost never see brahmavihara translated literally in English. *Brahmavihara* literally means "supreme abode," but the most common English translation I've seen is "the four sublime states." The most common Chinese translation literally means "the four immeasurables," almost certainly because ancient Chinese translators decided to use the synonym for brahmavihara, the Pali word *appamanna,* which literally means "boundless" or "immeasurable." I hope you're not immeasurably confused. The most amusing translation of *brahmavihara* I've come across is "best home." ("Where do you get your brahmavihara?" "At Best Home Depot.") Anyway, for the rest of this book, I will stick to the commonly used translation of "four sublime states."

The first question you might have about practice is, which one to do first? So many sublime states, so much goodness, so little time! Of the first three, one should definitely begin with loving-kindness, because it is easiest and most user-friendly. In fact, the friendly nature of loving-kindness is even reflected in its name. The original Pali word that gets translated to loving-kindness is *metta,* which is etymologically close to the Pali word for friend, *mitta.* That is why metta is sometimes translated to loving-friendliness.

Loving-kindness has many powerful benefits. The first benefit of loving-kindness is that it is highly conducive to joy. You may have already experienced it yourself with only a few seconds or minutes of doing the loving-kindness practices in this chapter. The effects of loving-kindness on emotions have also been investigated scientifically. A 2008 study, for example, led by preeminent psychologist Barbara Fredrickson showed that, "Participants who invested an hour or so each week practicing [loving-kindness meditation] enhanced a wide range of positive emotions in a wide range of situations, especially when interacting with others."[5] The study also reports, "The findings are clear cut: The practice of [loving-kindness meditation] led to shifts in people's daily experiences of a wide range of positive emotions, including love, joy, gratitude, contentment, hope, pride, interest, amusement, and awe." Another benefit, which is totally unsurprising, is if you're strong in loving-kindness, people tend to like you. The ancient texts claim that even animals tend to like you and behave favorably toward you if you are strong in loving-kindness.

More important, in mind training, loving-kindness is highly conducive to meditative concentration. One who is strong in loving-kindness can more easily settle and concentrate the mind. In fact, I know of meditation masters who use loving-kindness as their main vehicle for arriving at states of perfect meditative concentration. Perhaps most important, loving-kindness paves the way for the other three sublime states, so someone who is very strong in loving-kindness will find the other three sublime states requiring very little extra effort to cultivate. ("Buy loving-kindness now, and you'll get the other three sublime states for just $19.95! Shipping and handling charges may apply.")

All four sublime states are very beneficial. If you have to choose only one, definitely choose loving-kindness. Given its ease, friendliness, and awesome power, you can't go wrong with it.

If you do one thing in addition to loving-kindness, I recommend rejoicing in the inner goodness and altruistic deeds of yourself and others, mostly because it is easy to do and yields compellingly large benefit in proportion to the tiny effort required. All it takes is a few minutes of reflecting on and taking delight in the goodness and altruism of yourself or others in formal meditation, and a few moments of doing so in daily life, and this kind of altruistic joy can result in major mind-uplift.

If you do one more thing after that, definitely it should be compassion. Of the first three sublime states, compassion is the most potent. It is the one that directly addresses suffering right in its face, it is the one that motivates altruistic social action and heroic behavior, and it is the one that brings about the most selfless love. It is because of its potency that compassion is elevated to the status of the highest virtue in many schools in Buddhism. This stuff is hard-core. I most strongly recommend practicing compassion, and doing so *after* some foundation in loving-kindness is firmly established.

As for the last sublime state, equanimity, well, you have been cultivating it already. The seeds were planted when you took your first mindful breath. The roots grow every time you settle the mind into a state of ease and inner joy. You water the roots every time you incline the mind toward wholesome joy. In Chapter 7, we will talk about how we bring about the blossoming of equanimity.

Enemies Near and Far

When foraging for mushrooms in the wild, the biggest danger comes from picking a toxic mushroom that looks a lot like the edible mushroom you intended to pick. For example, if you're foraging for the delicious morel mushroom, the danger doesn't come from accidentally picking a death cap mushroom—they look very different from morels and you know to avoid them. The real danger comes from picking a false morel, which looks like a morel, except it is toxic. Hence, in foraging for mushrooms, the most important thing is to recognize the toxic look-alikes.

In the same way, every sublime state has one or more toxic look-alikes, which in the parlance of the traditional texts, are known as near enemies. Every sublime state also has one or more far enemies, which are the direct opposite states. We all already know to avoid the far enemies—it is the near enemies, due to their close resemblance to the sublime states, that cause the most problems. It's important to recognize the near enemies.

The far enemy of loving-kindness is ill will, especially strong ill will, as in hatred. Loving-kindness has two near enemies, both of which are often dominant in romantic relationships, which is why those relationships tend to go sour over time. The first is the type of affection that keeps you compulsively thirsting for more, almost like an addiction. In loving-kindness, the absence of the other person does not lead to pain, agitation, or thirst, because if it does, it is clinging, not loving-kindness. Loving-kindness is always wholesome. The second near enemy is conditional love, or affection that depends on whether the other person exists in a certain way, does certain things, or provides you with a certain set of sensory or ego pleasures. For example, if your tender loving feelings for him will fade if he is no longer successful and confident, or if your tender loving feelings for her will fizzle out if she is no longer beautiful, then no, that is not loving-kindness. Loving-kindness is always unconditional and selfless. Having said that, we should note that unconditional loving-kindness does not mean that we do not set boundaries to protect ourselves from harm. For example, if your husband is abusive, your loving-kindness should not stop you from getting a restraining order. You can wish for him to be happy, but you don't have to wish for him to be in your home.

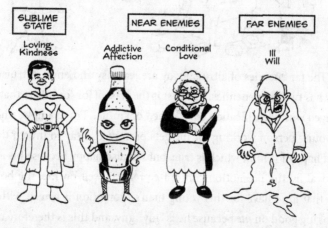

The far enemy of compassion is cruelty. Compassion has two near enemies. The first is grief born of despair. As Matthieu Ricard says, true compassion is based on the type of healthy sadness that inspires both a loving response and courageous action. In contrast, the type of grief that causes helplessness, despair, and powerlessness is unhealthy. It needs to be transformed into healthy sadness for compassion to properly function. The second near enemy of compassion is pity. To pity somebody necessarily (and often unconsciously) means you are putting yourself above that person, and that (often unconsciously and insidiously) reinforces an unhealthy ego. In contrast, compassion does not put you above or below the other person. Compassion is always selfless and ego-busting. It is also always wholesome.

The far enemies of altruistic joy are jealousy and envy. Altruistic joy has two near enemies. The first is the type of joy for others that is tinged with identification of "I," "me," or "mine." For example, when a young person working for me gets promoted, I say to myself that I'm happy for him, which is true, but I'm also happy because his approval by the promotion committee reflects well on me, the boss. So that joy I have for this young man's promotion is tinged with it looking good on *me* because he is "my" guy, and this is therefore not altruistic joy. The second near enemy of altruistic joy is rejoicing in the unwholesome joy of others (and also of self, for that matter).[6] If, for example, somebody experiences joy from abusing a narcotic, or somebody else is celebrating the joy of getting filthy rich by cheating little old ladies out of their life savings and/or causing a global financial meltdown, then no, rejoicing for them is not wholesome. The reason is the sources of their joy are contaminated with greed, ill will, or the seeds of future suffering for themselves and for others, making those sources unwholesome. To rejoice in joy from unwholesome sources is itself unwholesome, meta-unwholesome even. It is therefore not altruistic joy. Like loving-kindness and compassion, altruistic joy is always selfless and wholesome.

The far enemies of equanimity are mental factors that cause agitation in the mind, such as restlessness, anxiety, craving, and hatred. Equanimity has two near enemies. The first is disengagement, when we simply ignore what we do not want to see. The second near enemy of equanimity is apathy. With disengagement, a person ignores and doesn't see; with apathy, the person sees but doesn't care. In truth, equanimity both sees and cares. Remember that we practice equanimity alongside the other three sublime states, so it does see happiness and suffering, it cares about happiness and suffering (our own and others'), and at the same time, it involves calmness and clarity. Equanimity is unperturbed by all the pleasure and pain that passes through the mind. To equate equanimity with disengagement or apathy is like equating courage with safe distance. If we feel brave only when we are a safe distance away from danger, that is not courage. In the same way, if we feel calm only when we stop caring, that is not equanimity.

Once you learn to recognize the near enemies of loving-kindness, compassion, altruistic joy, and equanimity for what they really are, then you will not end up like one of those situations in a bad horror movie where the protagonist unknowingly marries the murderous evil twin of his true love, and he doesn't even know that she has a twin until near the end of the movie, by which time he is already trapped in a locked room with nothing to defend himself with except a deadly weapon somehow lying conveniently on the floor. You can avoid that fate.

So That's Why They're Called Heart Qualities

It turns out that the sublime states have a lot to do with the physical heart. Physiologically, we usually experience them in the region around the heart, which is why they are called heart qualities. In fact, the brain and the heart have close functional connections with each other, a phenomenon fancily called neurocardiac coupling. In the experience of the sublime states, this brain-heart connection shows up especially strong. The main conduit is the vagus nerve, which also helps regulate heart rate, blood pressure, glucose levels, immune response, and many other things. In a state of kindness or compassion, for example, your vagus nerve gets activated. One thing that does is it relaxes the muscles around the heart, so you experience the physical sensation of "opening of the heart." So the experience of "kindness opening my heart" has a neurological explanation, and some of you thought it was just hippie bullshit.

Frequent activation of the vagus nerve turns out to be very good for your physical health. If you often have thoughts of kindness, compassion, and altruistic joy, you activate the vagus nerve a lot, and after a while, your vagal tone improves.[7] High vagal tone is correlated with a healthy heart, while low vagal tone predicts heart failure and mortality after heart attacks. High vagal tone increases resilience to stress and the likelihood of positive emotional experiences such as joy, interest, serenity, and hope.[8] It also shows up socially. People with strong vagal tone develop richer relationships and, fascinating, are more likely to be trusted instinctively by other people.[9] Somehow, we know to trust people with strong vagal tone. As if all that is not good enough, people with high vagal tones also demonstrate superior cognitive flexibility, including better working memory and directed attention. They also show fewer negative responses to environmental stressors and show greater self-regulatory capacity.[10]

Many years ago, when the Dalai Lama first became interested in helping scientists study Buddhist meditation scientifically, he invited a group of Tibetan Buddhist monks in a monastery in India to become experimental subjects. Of course, Tibetan Buddhist monks sort of don't say no to . . . er . . . invitations from the Dalai Lama. A team of Western scientists, including the distinguished Chilean neuroscientist Francisco Varela, visited the monks with their equipment and, through an interpreter, tried to explain to the monks what they were attempting to do. They told the monks that they wanted to measure compassion, and to demonstrate, Francisco put on an EEG cap that measures electrical activity on the surface of the brain. All the monks then burst out laughing. The scientists assumed the monks were laughing because Francisco looked silly with an EEG cap on. But no, that's not why they were laughing. The scientists soon found out that the monks were all laughing because they thought the Westerners were being silly, because if they wanted to measure compassion, they should be measuring the heart, not the head. Duh. The scientists were aghast and attributed it to "cultural differences," implying that the monks didn't know what they were talking about. Many years later, with the benefit of new scientific understanding into the neurocardiac effects of compassion, we now know that the monks were right. Never underestimate a roomful of laughing Buddhist monks.

I can't figure out why they're laughing. Must be some cultural difference.

Selfless Love, a Short Poem

I would like to end this chapter with a poem that beautifully captures the spirit of the sublime states. It was shared with me by the revered Catholic Benedictine monk Brother David Steindl-Rast, best known for his teachings on gratefulness. I see Brother David as a real brother, so the most convenient thing about Brother David is that he has a self-documenting name, at least to me.

Brother David told me of this poem that describes the relationship between self and other as selfless love gains strength. For Brother David, "other" here refers to God, but it may also refer to anything else: the universe, Nirvana, or other people.

> In the beginning, there is only self, there is no other.
> And then, there is self, and there is other.
> Later on, self and other are one, there is no separation.
> Finally, there is no self, there is only other.

Happiness Is Full of Crap

Working with Emotional Pain

Great spiritual teachers tend to be funny people, and sometimes, they even talk shit. I know of at least two analogies of the meditative mind that involve excrement. In one, the mind is compared to a piece of pure gold hidden inside a big ball of cattle dung. The gold represents the mind in its underlying nature, perfect and happy, while the cattle dung represents the mental conditions that hinder the perfect, happy nature of the mind. The gold is already there—it does not have to be created, so all we have to do to get to the gold is wash away the cattle dung. Similarly, happiness is already there, so we don't have to create the mental conditions for happiness; we merely have to remove the mental conditions that hinder happiness.

The other analogy is the story of a man stepping in a big pile of dog poop on his way home. The soles of his shoes are now full of dog poop, and he can either walk into the house with those shoes and dirty his carpet with dog poop, or he can wash his shoes in his backyard, thereby using the dog poop to fertilize the soil. The dog poop represents the suffering (the bad shit) in our lives. When bad things happen to us, we can choose to either let our suffering permanently stink up our lives, like the man who tracks dog poop through his house, or let it promote our spiritual growth, like the man who turns the dog poop into lawn fertilizer.

In life, painful emotions are unavoidable. We grow old, we get sick, we experience physical pain, and we face death (our own and that of our loved ones). Also, very often, life forces us to be with things that we greatly dislike, or it prevents us from getting what we desperately want, or we lose what we have that is dear to us. In every case, some emotional pain is unavoidable. Even Matthieu Ricard, the "happiest man in the world," with sixty thousand hours of mind training and counting, tells me that it is impossible to be joyful all the time, because pain and difficulties in life are inevitable and there is so much suffering everywhere. Therefore, as we train ourselves in the art of joy, it is equally important to also learn suffering. The meditator who learns joy without learning suffering is like the fighter who learns to attack without learning to defend—her training is grossly incomplete.

In this chapter, we will use inner peace, inner joy, inner clarity, and loving-kindness to work with suffering. I suggest there are three steps in doing that: an **attentional step,** an **affective step,** and a **cognitive step.**

These steps are useful in all situations involving emotional pain, whether you feel sad, or angry, or humiliated, or betrayed, or hateful, or any other bad shit. We will discuss these steps in some detail. Sometimes, however, our difficulties are so intense and the emotional pain is so severe that even these three steps fail. In times like those, we practice the art of suffering.

Step 1 in Working with Emotional Pain: The Attentional Step

The first step in working with emotional pain can be summarized in three words: **calm the mind.**

Whenever I am afflicted with a painful emotion, the very first thing I do is calm the mind. I do this by deploying my attention. I turn my mindfulness on to full power, and then I bring attention to my breath, away from the thoughts that are fueling my pain. Sometimes it takes a second, sometimes it takes minutes, but either way, simply by bringing gentle but intense attention to the breath, I calm my mind.

Back in Chapter 2, we talked about how this works. Bringing attention to the breath calms the mind in two ways, one physiological and one psychological. Physiologically, attending to the breath makes it slower and deeper and thereby stimulates the vagus nerve, which then launches the relaxation response. Psychologically, attending to the breath intensely brings the mind to the present, away from past and future, and so temporarily frees the mind from regret (about the past) and worry (about the future). Under normal conditions, it is easy to calm the mind by attending to the breath, but it is harder to do so under stressful conditions, precisely when you need it the most. Fortunately, if you practice it a lot under normal conditions, then in times of need, in the midst of emotional pain, you will be able to activate it instinctively. It is like going to the gym a lot to build up your strength—if you then find yourself hanging from a cliff, your physical strength is available to you to pull yourself up. Similarly, training the "muscles" of your attention will make your attentional powers available to you when you find yourself in very painful situations.

How helpful is calming the mind in the midst of pain? Let me illustrate with an ancient story.

Once upon a time in India, there was a woman called Patacara. She was the beloved daughter of a wealthy merchant. When she was sixteen years old, she fell in love with one of her father's servants, and they eloped.

The young couple lived a hard life in a village far away. When Patacara became pregnant, she begged her husband to take her to her parents' house in the town of Savatthi to give birth. He refused.

So one day, while her husband was away, she made the trip unilaterally. Her husband managed to catch up with her and pleaded with her to return home, but she refused. Before they reached Savatthi, though, she gave birth to a son.

Having no more reason to go to Savatthi, they turned back and headed home to the village. When Patacara became pregnant again, she made the same request to her husband, and again he refused. So once again, while he was away, she made the trip to

Savatthi without him, taking her son along. Once again, the husband caught up with her, tried persuading her to turn back, and once again, she refused.

On this day, there was an unseasonably heavy thunderstorm. The husband set out to chop some wood to make Patacara a shelter. While doing that, he was killed by a poisonous snake. Meanwhile, Patacara gave birth to a second son. In the morning, she found her husband lying dead. Distraught, she blamed herself for his death. She continued on her journey to Savatthi and was blocked by a river that was swollen due to the heavy rain. Unable to cross with both children at once, she left the older one on the shore and carried the baby across, planning to come back for the older one. Halfway on her return, an eagle took the baby away for food. Patacara screamed at the eagle. When the older boy heard the screams, he thought his mother was calling for him, so he entered the river and was swept away by the strong current. Totally distraught, Patacara continued her journey to Savatthi and found out her parents and her only brother had all been killed after their house collapsed during the storm the previous day. In a single day, Patacara lost everybody dear to her. In extreme pain, she went stark crazy, tore up her own clothes and started wandering the streets of Savatthi half naked.

It's all very dramatic, but I'm trying to figure out where to put the song and dance numbers.

Eventually, Patacara wandered into the grove where the Buddha was staying. When the Buddha saw her, the first thing he said to her was, "Friend, calm your mind." Patacara responded. She calmed her mind, regained her senses, and suddenly realized she was half naked. Somebody offered her a set of robes, and she quickly wrapped them around herself. Her healing had begun. Patacara eventually gained enlightenment and became one of the most noted female Buddhist monastics.

I learned of this story a long time ago when I was a novice meditator. It was so stark, I have never forgotten it, and the lesson stuck permanently in my mind, which is that no matter how bad the pain is, no matter how horrible the situation is always, first and foremost, try to calm the mind.

Step 2 in Working with Emotional Pain: The Affective Step

This step deals with the feeling of the emotionally painful experience. The previous attentional step is necessary, but often insufficient. It is necessary because without first calming the mind, you can't begin to cope with the difficult emotion, but it is insufficient because, quite often, the emotion will come back soon after you stop actively calming the mind. When that happens, this affective step is required.

There are two parts to this step. The first is to be willing to experience joy in the midst of emotional pain. The second is to be willing to experience the emotional pain itself.

Willingness to Experience Joy

Does it surprise you to hear that it is possible to access moments of pure, unadulterated joy in the middle of emotional pain? It surprised me. In the previous chapters, we talked about easing into joy, attending to joy, and uplifting the mind with joy—in other words, the ability to access joy on demand under normal (non-painful) circumstances, both in meditation and in daily life. The fact that it is possible to access joy on demand in those circumstances was surprising enough to me. So I was astonished to discover that it is sometimes possible, to some degree, even under very painful circumstances.

As I developed more skill at accessing joy in meditation, I realized I could do it even when I had a crappy day and I was feeling sad, angry, or disheartened. Sometimes, all I have to do is calm the mind and, lo and behold, the mind eases into joy, sometimes for minutes, sometimes for the rest of the day. At other times, I meditate on loving-kindness and this uplifts the mind into joy, again, sometimes just for a few minutes, sometimes for much longer.

I learned two things from this experience. First, I learned, as the masters have taught over thousands of years, that **peace and joy are the default states of mind.** They don't have to be created—they just need to be accessed. The mind in its peaceful and joyous state is like the moon—the emotions that hinder peace and joy such as sadness and hatred are like dark clouds in the sky obscuring the moon. The dark clouds only obscure the moon, not destroy it, and the mere absence of the dark clouds will reveal the moon. Similarly, the painful emotions merely obscure the default peace and joy of mind, not destroy them, so the mere absence, or parting, of the painful emotions will reveal mental peace and joy. To access peace and joy, we don't have to do anything except let go of the painful emotions that obscure them. Second, I learned that even though peace and joy are the default states of mind, accessing them is not always easy, and sometimes, is not even possible. And even if I can access them, I cannot always maintain that access in the midst of painful emotions. Sometimes, the access lasts no more than a minute or even just a few seconds. On difficult days, it is like doing a handstand: just doing it is hard; maintaining it for more than a minute is even harder. On impossible days, it is like trying to see a moon through clouds in a thunderstorm—one simply has no choice but to hunker down and wait for the weather to change.

The mind accessing joy in the midst of great emotional difficulties is illustrated by a beautiful Zen parable involving a tiger and a strawberry.

The Tiger and the Strawberry

Once upon a time, a man was being chased by a hungry tiger.

As he ran, he fell off a steep cliff, but just as he was falling, he managed to grab hold of a branch growing on the edge of the cliff. That stopped his fall. He was alive, for now, but he was also stuck in a precarious situation. He could not let go of the branch, because if he did, he would fall a thousand feet to his death. He also could not climb back up because the tiger was waiting for him at the top of the cliff only a few feet above him.

As he was hanging on precariously, two mice appeared and started gnawing away at the very branch he was holding on to for dear life.

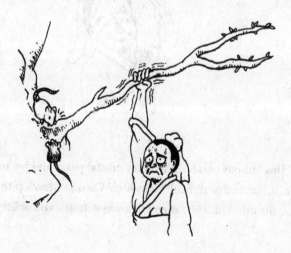

Just then, the man noticed a strawberry near to him.

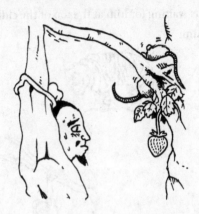

He reached out, plucked the strawberry, and ate it. It was delicious.

This famous parable illustrates mental peace and joy in the middle of impossible difficulties in life. When we develop the skills to ease the mind into joy, attend to joy as it arises, and uplift the mind, then even in the middle of great difficulty, we may *sometimes* find moments when we can access peace and joy. Each moment of peace and joy in the midst of emotional pain is like the occasional oasis in a vast desert. The oases let you cross the desert. In the same way, having access to moments of peace and joy lets you navigate emotional difficulties, even when they are vast.

That was a parable. How does it look in real life? I learned this from a Nobel Peace Prize winner named Rigoberta Menchú Tum.

Just Because You're In Pain Doesn't Mean You Can't Be Joyful

Rigoberta was awarded the Nobel Peace Prize in 1992 for her life's work in promoting human rights. When I met her, I found her to be exactly what you'd expect of a stereotypical Nobel Peace Prize winner: she was wise, kind, and joyful. She is friendly to everyone and treats everyone with kindness. She gives people a huge smile and warm hugs. She is bursting with joy. Right beneath the surface, however, there is a huge reservoir of pain. Her father was burned alive. Her mother was raped and tortured before she died. Her brother was murdered. She lost her youngest son. She watched many thousands of people oppressed, tortured, and murdered. When I realized the amount of pain she was holding, I wanted to cry. One of the signs of true greatness is the ability to hold a large amount of pain, not just with courage and equanimity, but also with kindness, compassion, and joy. Rigoberta showed me what greatness looks like. I was moved.

While I was onstage with Rigoberta, I asked her where that greatness comes from. Is it something she was born with, or is it something she grew into? She said it comes from deep spiritual practice, and in her case, practices from her own Mayan tradition. (She is from Guatemala.) Offstage, while we were taking a walk, she pointed to me and said, "You know, my Mayan spirituality, not so different from your Buddhist spirituality." We both laughed.

The meeting with Rigoberta led me to an important insight concerning the relationship between joy and overwhelming pain. I realized that joy and pain can exist solidly side by side. When joy is much stronger than pain, the joy can displace the pain, but when the pain is so strong it cannot be displaced, then the joy can exist alongside the pain without displacing it or dissolving it away. There have been dark periods in my life when I have suffered tremendous emotional pain, and at the same time, thanks to my mental training, I have been able to access genuine joy intermittently in the midst of the pain. Sometimes, those two things, the pain that was so unbearable that I wanted to die and the joy that filled up my entire mind, appeared just minutes apart from each other. Until I met Rigoberta, it made no sense to me at all. Why did the joy not dissolve away the pain? Conversely, if the pain was so bad, why did it not dissolve away the joy? I thought I was going crazy (more than usual, I mean).

Rigoberta's example had answered my question. She showed me that when pain is overwhelming, joy does not dissolve away the pain. Instead, it becomes a skillful container for the pain, limiting its damage and allowing the healing process to work. It is a little like putting a cast around your leg when you have a serious fracture. It prevents further damage and allows the leg to heal over time. Rigoberta demonstrated to me, by her own example, how one can hold immense pain, gently, with joy.

The mutual insolubility of joy and pain has another important consequence, which my very dear friend and fifteen-time Nobel Peace Prize nominee Dawn Engle puts very nicely: "Just because you're in pain doesn't mean you cannot be joyful."

The key lesson, my friends: never be afraid to experience joy in the midst of great pain.

Oh, stop complaining! Dawn Engle says just because you're in pain doesn't mean you can't be joyful.

Willingness to Experience the Emotional Pain

Complementing the willingness to experience joy in the midst of emotional pain is the willingness to experience the emotional pain itself.

Emotional pain has two components: the feelings experienced in the body and the thoughts that spark and then fuel the continuation of those feelings. We experience emotion in the body, so we must work with them in the body. Difficult emotions always involve unpleasant sensations in the body. For example, when I'm distressed, my face tenses up, I may feel the urge to shed tears, and I have an extremely unpleasant feeling in my chest and stomach. My heart pounds, my body tenses up, I feel sick in the stomach, and I feel a very uncomfortable constriction in my chest. The willingness to experience emotional pain is, in large part, the willingness to experience great unpleasantness in the body.

There are four steps to working with painful emotions in the body. The first is to clearly perceive that these **emotions are just unpleasant**

sensations in the body. This anguish I am feeling is simply a terribly unpleasant sensation in my face, my throat, my shoulders, my chest, and my stomach. It is on the same level as a toothache—they are both simply terribly unpleasant bodily sensations, that is all. The second step is to recognize the central role played by aversion. When we experience an unpleasant bodily sensation, the sensation leads to perception, the perception leads to aversion, and the aversion leads to suffering. We don't like feeling this way. We think we *can't stand* to feel this way. The most important insight here is that **aversion is the proximate cause of suffering.** Therefore, to reduce or eliminate suffering, the point of attack is aversion: the more this aversion can be reduced, the less suffering one experiences, despite the sensation and perception of emotional pain. In other words, the feeling (sensation and perception) is the same, but the feeling about the feeling is different. The third step is to apply the **first antidote to aversion: loving-kindness.** By seeing the painful emotion clearly for what it is (bodily sensations) and then applying loving-kindness both to the emotion and to the self, one begins to soothe the pain.

There is an old Indian parable that illustrates this point in the form of a fun story. Once upon a time, there was a monster called Anger Monster that fed on anger. He found plenty of food in the human realm, and he lived well.

One day, on his vacation, he traveled to the heavenly realm and, quite by accident, discovered that even the gods get angry, and their anger tasted heavenly.

He decided he wanted to feast on the anger of the gods, but how does one get plenty of gods angry all at once? Anger Monster discovered that Sakra, the king of gods, was away, perhaps on some sort of business trip, so Anger Monster decided to sit on Sakra's throne. When the gods found out, they got angry at him. They all came to Sakra's throne, screamed at Anger Monster, and demanded that he leave. Anger Monster fed on all their anger, and better still, thanks to all the heavenly vitamins and minerals in the anger of the gods, every time Anger Monster fed on a god's anger, he grew bigger. Soon, he was so big that none of the gods could do anything to him. Some time later, Sakra returned from his trip to find a ginormous monster sitting on his throne.

Oh no, what to do? Fortunately, the heavenly king was wise. First, he clearly saw Anger Monster for what he was, and then he treated the monster with loving-kindness.

He spoke kindly and lovingly to Anger Monster, and with every word he spoke, the monster got a little smaller. Eventually, Anger Monster shrunk to the size of a pea, and the wise king gently took him off the throne.

If it is too hard to bring up loving-kindness toward yourself or your situation, try doing it for somebody for whom it is easy for you to have unconditional love, because that feeling alone will go some way in soothing emotional pain.

The fourth and final step to working with painful emotions in the body is to apply the **second antidote to aversion: equanimity.** Having applied loving-kindness, I try to apply equanimity by keeping my attention on the level of sensation as much as possible, just watching the sensations in my body. Every now and then, I remind myself, these emotions that I feel, they are simply sensations in my body—**these emotions are not me.** In addition, those thoughts that come alongside these bodily sensations, they are simply thoughts—**these thoughts are also not me.** The mind is like the sky, and thoughts are like clouds in the sky—the clouds are not the sky. Similarly, these thoughts are not the mind—they are not me. By coping in this way, seeing emotions simply as bodily sensations, and thoughts simply as a stream of mental phenomena, I allow all these feelings and all these thoughts to occupy my body and mind. I allow them to stay as long as they want, cause as much pain as they want. All I do is watch them with equanimity. Some meditators call it "sitting in the fire."

Jonathan Berent, a director at Google (whom we met in the introduction, setting his watch to remind him to breathe), describes how equanimity changed his experience of pain during a particularly difficult time:

> My journey to joy on demand has not been without some really serious things to deal with. A year ago, my wife and I learned that she would need to have three separate, unrelated surgeries. One of these required six weeks off work to recover and an all-liquid diet during that time. Another, to remove a benign cyst from under her arm, meant she couldn't drive for at least a month. I had been practicing mindfulness meditation for only about six months at the time, but even with this limited amount of practice, I was able to witness the stress, the frustration, and the fear arise in the mind. I soon realized, when I let my mind identify with these emotions, I was not present for my wife. However, when I simply witnessed them as clouds in the sky of my mind, I found a deeper reality behind them. Compassion. When I let go of my fear, my thoughts of "God, why all this? Why all at once?" I found I could love my wife with a level of depth and empathy she had not experienced before.
>
> Now all three surgeries and recovery periods are behind us. My wife recently said, "I think this year of marriage has been the best." Holy shit. And I hundred-percent agree with her.[1]

In summary, the affective step begins with the willingness to experience joy in the midst of emotional pain, allowing the joy to surface whenever and wherever it wants. After that, cultivate the willingness to experience the emotional pain itself. Do this by perceiving the affective experience of the emotional pain in its component parts (bodily sensations, thoughts, and aversion) clearly, just as they are. Then, apply loving-kindness to yourself as much as possible; then sit with whatever bodily sensations and thoughts you experience, doing so in stillness and equanimity, allowing all those bodily sensations and thoughts to come and go, knowing that they are not you.

Step 3 in Working with Emotional Pain: The Cognitive Step

The cognitive step in working with emotional pain involves rethinking the situation that brought about the emotional pain. It is about taking the skillful perspective, seeing the big picture without our objectivity being clouded by afflictive emotions. It very often involves reframing or reinterpreting the meaning of the situation with two things: objectivity and compassion. This step is often necessary because if we only take the attentional and affective steps, the underlying causes of the emotional pain likely remain unresolved, and unresolved issues often strike back. The cognitive step is about dealing with underlying issues in the most objective and compassionate way that, to the extent possible, benefits everybody.

Cognitive reappraisal is often required for one simple reason: our perception of reality is often seriously flawed. First, the information we gather is necessarily incomplete because there is a severe limit to how many things we can perceive and pay attention to at any one time. How severe? In one of the most famous experiments in psychology, researchers from Harvard University asked people to watch a short video in which six people pass basketballs around and had them count the number of passes made by the three people in white shirts. At some point in the video, somebody in a gorilla suit walked right into the middle of the action, faced the camera, and then left. Fully half the people who watched the video and counted the passes missed the gorilla.[2]

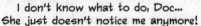

I don't know what to do, Doc... She just doesn't notice me anymore!

To make things worse, we often unconsciously fill in the missing information with our imagination and then our brains don't take the trouble to differentiate between imagination and facts. In other words, our brains often make crap up and then pretend the crap is real. Even worse, our brains have a strong negative bias. They perceive things that affect us negatively much more strongly than things that affect us positively. For example, imagine you are an author and your first book has a hundred reviews on Amazon.com, of which seventy-five are five-star reviews, and only two are one-star reviews. Guess which reviews you pay the most attention to? No, I don't know where I got this example—I must have made it up.

One major consequence of our seriously flawed perception of reality is that it creates a lot of unnecessary suffering, and it does so in at least three ways. First, it damages our relationships. We often judge others by jumping to conclusions about their intentions based on the effects their actions have on us, which often are more negative than their actual intentions. For example, our feelings are hurt and we assume the person meant to hurt our feelings. That hurts our feelings even more, not to mention leaves us thinking, "That person is a jerk." Clearly, this hurts our relationship with that person, who may in fact be horrified to know our feelings were hurt.

Second, the way we judge ourselves tends to be far more negative than the facts can justify. I realized I suffer from this myself in a comical way. Whenever I do something important, there is always a part of me convinced I'm going to mess it up. One time, I was about to deliver a major speech, and I told my best friend, Rich, "I'm so going to fruit this up" (which means to mess things up bad, in case you have to ask). Being my best friend, Rich got sick of hearing me saying over and over again that I'm going to fruit something up, so he decided to appeal to the engineer in me and asked me, "Show me the data: when was the last time in a similar situation you seriously fruited up?" I had no answer. He was right—the data did not justify the degree of the negativity with which I saw myself.

Freeze,
Motherfruiter!

Third, our seriously flawed perception of reality leads us to be far less happy than our life circumstances justify because we tend to downplay the positives and overplay the negatives in our lives. As the comedian Louis C. K. famously said to Conan O'Brien, "Everything is amazing right now, and nobody's happy."[3]

Again, I have a comical example. Many years ago, a young person from Singapore received her first credit card, which was kind of a big deal for her because personal credit control used to be very tight in Singapore, so young people her age didn't usually earn enough to qualify for credit cards. When she opened up the envelope, she was very excited, but it only took a few seconds for her excited smile to turn into a frown. Why? Because the pretty new credit card had some light scratches. Her brain had quickly downplayed the joy of her hard-earned financial victory and overplayed the negativity of a few light scratches. She asked me what to do, so I said to her, "Do you know how big the universe is? The nearest star to ours is four light-years away. If we travel at the speed of light, it'll be four years before we reach another star. Our galaxy is a hundred thousand light-years in diameter, containing millions and millions of stars. The nearest spiral galaxy to ours, the Andromeda Galaxy, is 2.5 million light-years away. If we travel at light speed from the edge of our galaxy to that galaxy, we can travel for 2.5 million years, twenty-five times longer than the entire existence of *Homo sapiens,* and all we'll encounter is space. Nothing but space. And that's just the distance between two closest galaxies. There are probably millions of these galaxies in the universe. The universe is unimaginably huge. And back here on earth, one woman is concerned about light scratches on her credit card." She laughed and was no longer upset.

Given all that, it is skillful to cognitively reappraise every situation that causes us suffering because it is very likely that at least some large percentage of our suffering originates from some amount of imperfection in perception. I suggest reappraising in six ways:

1. With kindness and compassion to others. If your emotional pain is caused by the actions of another person, it is best to do loving-kindness toward that same person, reminding yourself that this person is like me in three ways: she is human, just like me; she wants to be happy, just like me; she wants to be free from suffering, just like me. Keep that in mind and give her the benefit of the doubt.

2. With kindness and compassion to yourself. See yourself in the eyes of your caring best friend. Your best friend would very likely tell you things are not nearly as bad as you think, and objectively, he or she is likely to be more accurate than you. Keep that in mind and give yourself the benefit of the doubt.

3. By not believing everything you think. Remember that the brain doesn't usually differentiate between imagination and fact. Keep that in mind and always be willing to be wrong.

4. By seeing the long term and the big picture. In the long term, every mistake is an opportunity for learning and growth. It is also good to be always aware that someday we will die—it puts things in proper perspective.

5. By seeing everything for the miracle that it is. Zen master Thich Nhat Hanh poetically says, "The real miracle is not to walk either on water or in thin air, but to walk on earth. Every day we are engaged in a miracle which we don't even recognize: a blue sky, white clouds, green leaves, the black, curious eyes of a child—our own two eyes. All is a miracle."[4] Or, as Louis C. K. put it, less poetically but more humorously

when he talked about people complaining on airplanes, "Did you partake in the miracle of human flight, you noncontributing zero? You got to fly! It's amazing! Everybody on every plane should just constantly be going 'Oh my God! Wow!' You're flying! You're sitting in a chair, in the sky!"[5]

6. With joy and humor. Because, like, why not?

Being Very Good at Working With Emotional Pain

The three steps for working with emotional pain (the attentional step, the affective step, and the cognitive step) work best when executed in that order. Without the attentional step to calm the mind, the other two steps are impossible, but that attentional step is usually only the beginning. The affective step is often necessary, but it doesn't always resolve the underlying causes of the problem. The cognitive step is usually needed to resolve underlying issues or the problem will keep coming back, but this step cannot be taken when judgment is still clouded by emotional pain, and therefore it needs to rely on the other two steps.

What is it like to be very good at doing this? I can think of at least two people who excel at working with emotional pain, both of whom are Zen teachers, one of whom I know in person and the other being one of the greatest Zen masters in history. The one I know is a dear friend whom I admire, a meditation teacher deeply influenced by Zen, Soryu Forall. One thing I most admire about him is the way he helps people in pain. In his job as a meditation teacher, people bring their pain to him all the time. When somebody tells him how she is suffering, Soryu makes himself fully vulnerable, opens his own body and mind to all her suffering, and for a moment, he suffers exactly like she does. From that low point, he allows his practice to resolve the suffering in himself, and as he does, he describes what is happening in such a way that the other person understands how to do it. I'm awed by his methodology. It is, to me, the most difficult and also the most effective way to help others in pain. It is also counter to my own training. Many years ago, when I received some training in counseling, I was told to never take on the other person's pain because if I did that, all I would do was transfer some of the other person's pain to myself, so she would feel better, but I would feel worse, and there would be no net gain in the world. In contrast, Soryu makes himself as vulnerable as he can and is utterly without resistance to the pain. He is totally open to it. He doesn't resist its arising or its passing.

Why does Soryu do this? He told me it was because of a conversation he had with a Zen master midway through his Zen training that changed his life. It started when he asked the master an innocent question, "Does a buddha ever feel sad?" That is, of course, a silly question for a Buddhist. Every Buddhist knows that the answer is no. A buddha is one who has perfected the mind in every way and is therefore totally immune from all suffering, so obviously, a buddha will never feel sad. The master offered Soryu a surprising answer. He said, "When a buddha meets a sad person, the buddha becomes sad for one moment. Why is this? Because if he didn't, the sad person would have no way to meet the buddha." From that day on, Soryu decided he would not shield himself from the suffering of other people. He would receive their suffering and work his way out of that suffering together with them, because if he isn't willing to suffer with them, he would not be able to help them. He asks himself, "If I am not willing and able to escape from this suffering, how can I tell them how to?"

Soryu shows the courage of compassion, but more important, he demonstrates his confidence in the practice. He is willing to descend into the depths of pain because he is confident of being able to fly back out thanks to the strength of his practice. What he practices is similar to what you have learned in this book—the only difference is he has put in a lot more hours (Soryu has clocked about twenty-five thousand hours of lifetime meditation practice at the time I'm writing this). Soryu tells me that for him, "It is as if the experience of suffering is the experience of love, and of the joy that comes from directly experiencing the purification that arises from and returns to love."[6] As you gain more practice, you will begin to find that the same practices that help you access joy on demand can help you navigate the suffering in life, and very soon, you will begin to develop the same confidence in yourself.

Another example of what it is like to be very good at working with emotional pain comes from a story I read in the 1957 classic book *Zen Flesh, Zen Bones.* I read it when I was nineteen or twenty, and it awed me so much, it pulled me toward the practice (which I finally picked up at twenty-one). The story is an account of a pivotal incident in the life of the great Japanese Zen master Hakuin Ekaku (1686–1768), one of the most important Zen masters in Japanese history. Before this incident, Hakuin was already a locally well-known and highly respected Zen master, but after the incident, he was propelled to widespread fame. The story is beautifully rendered in *Zen Flesh, Zen Bones* with the title, "Is That So?"

Is That So?

A beautiful Japanese girl whose parents owned a food store lived near him. Suddenly, without any warning, her parents discovered she was with child.

This made her parents angry. She would not confess who the man was, but after much harassment at last named Hakuin.

In great anger the parents went to the master. "Is that so?" was all he would say.

After the child was born it was brought to Hakuin. By this time he had lost his reputation, which did not trouble him, but he took very good care of the child. He obtained milk from his neighbors and everything else the child needed.

A year later the girl-mother could stand it no longer. She told her parents the truth—that the real father of the child was a young man who worked in the fishmarket.

The mother and father of the girl at once went to Hakuin to ask forgiveness, to apologize at length, and to get the child back again.

Hakuin was willing. In yielding the child, all he said was: "Is that so?"[7]

Your Honor, the witness has responded to every question with "Is that so?" Permission to treat him as hostile.

Failure Is Not an Option, It Comes Preinstalled

The three-step formula in this chapter for working with emotional pain works most of the time but may not work all the time for you. The reason is the current depth of your practice may not yet be consummate with the magnitude of the suffering you face. Higher magnitudes of suffering often require a deeper level of practice to overcome. For example, let's say you have developed the skills to calm your mind when dealing with unreasonable customers. Previously, you'd grit your teeth and pretend to smile, but now, thanks to the training in this book, you are able to deal with them with perfect calmness and joy (you're welcome!). All your coworkers will be in awe of your cool, but that doesn't mean nothing will ever throw you off ever again. An event that causes a much higher magnitude of suffering, such as a cancer diagnosis, might still throw you into depression. And even after enough training to stay calm and joyful in the face of a cancer diagnosis, there might still be events that cause more suffering than you're able to deal with, such as finding out that your wife cheated on you.

A good analogy for this phenomenon is juggling. If you trained yourself to juggle three balls, it doesn't automatically mean you can juggle four balls. It takes you some practice to go from three to four balls, and then four to five, and so on, because each additional ball requires more skill. To expect a meditator with the ability to calm his or her mind

in a three-ball situation to have no trouble with a seven-ball problem
is not realistic.

To make matters worse, there is always a delay between developing awareness of affliction and developing the ability to resolve
it. For example, let's say you have a tendency to behave in certain
ways that get you into trouble. At first, you are unaware of it. After
some hours of mindfulness meditation, you begin to see how your
unskillful mental inclinations set you up for the type of behavior
that gets you into trouble, but to your horror, you find yourself unable to stop the behavior, even though you can clearly see the harm
it is causing. It is like watching yourself drive a car right into a wall
and not being able to step on the brakes. It is only after more (sometimes much more) practice that you learn to correct those unskillful
mental inclinations and change your behavior. The time between
being able to see the unskillfulness of the mind and resulting behaviors, and developing the necessary mental skills to do different, feels
horrible. During this period, you are likely to blame yourself and feel
like a failure. Here is a parable, inspired by the beautiful poem titled
Autobiography in Five Short Chapters written by singer, songwriter,
actress, and author Portia Nelson, that captures this phenomenon:

Day 1: I walk down the street. There is a deep hole in the sidewalk.
I do not see the hole. I walk right in.

Day 2: I walk down the same street. I see the deep hole in the sidewalk. I walk right in.

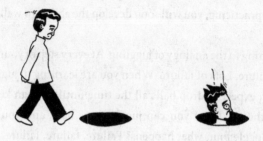

Day 3: I walk down the same street. I see the deep hole in the sidewalk. I walk around it.

The hardest day is Day 2. On Day 2, you can clearly see the hole in the sidewalk, and you can clearly see yourself walking right into it, and still, you are unable to stop yourself. But Day 2 is a prerequisite for Day 3. Only when you can clearly see how you fail will you be able to overcome the causes of those failures. So when you find yourself in Day 2, know that this is a natural progression toward Day 3 and if you keep practicing, you will soon develop the ability to walk around the hole.

Returning to the analogy of juggling. At every step of your growth, expect failure. Lots of failure. When you are learning to juggle three balls, you expect to drop balls all the time until you can keep three balls in the air. Once you can juggle three balls and you want to learn to juggle four, what happens? Failure, failure, failure. You will keep dropping balls as you practice until you gain the new ability. Eventually, you have no problem juggling four balls. If you decide to go for five, what then? Yes, failure, failure, failure, until you acquire the new skill.

When you are growing, it often feels like you are failing all the time, but I encourage you to look back at your journey every now and then to see how far you have come. For example, while you are dropping balls all over the place in your practice to juggle five, think back on your progress from two to three to four. At every step, you told yourself how great it would be to juggle one more ball, and at every step, you eventually succeeded. Understand that failure is an integral part of the growth process. Do not just see the failure—also see the growth. When you do, you will experience the joy of growing.

The Art of Suffering Is Love

What if your suffering is so intense that it completely overwhelms your ability to work with it? In that case, you need to learn the Art of Suffering.

A few years ago, as my meditation practice matured, I reached a point where my access to inner peace and inner joy had become so strong that I was quite good at overcoming suffering. Whenever I experienced suffering, I calmed my mind, I activated joy, and because this foundation was so firm, I could take the attentional, affective, and cognitive steps in dealing with emotional pain quite easily. And that became a problem. How? It created a big blind spot in my training. The great Zen master Thich Nhat Hanh teaches something called the Art of Suffering, and I never really learned it. I was like the kung fu fighter who was so good at blocking punches, he never developed the skill to roll with a punch, so on the occasion that an incoming punch was so powerful he was unable to block it, he got completely knocked out. And that happened to me. There was a time in my life when my suffering was so completely overwhelming, my skill at accessing calmness and joy was not strong enough to overcome it, so I couldn't even get on the steps. I was helpless.

During that period, I was very lucky to spend three days with the master, Thich Nhat Hanh, himself. He taught me to suffer skillfully. I learned the Art of Suffering. And then I realized what was missing from my practice.

From my (probably imperfect) understanding of Thich Nhat Hanh's teaching, there are three steps in suffering skillfully:

1. Don't think, just feel. As much as possible, just feel the present-moment sensations in the body. In the words of Thich Nhat Hanh, "Come home to yourself, come home to the present moment."

2. Cradle with tenderness. Figuratively cradle the self in pain like a mother cradles her crying baby. The mother doesn't know why the baby is crying, but she cradles the baby anyway,

and just by doing that, the baby feels better. Similarly, treat the self in pain like a baby and cradle it tenderly with love.

3. Cultivate compassion from this suffering. Compassion arises from understanding suffering. Suffering is like mud, compassion is like lotus, and you need the mud to grow the lotus. So understand the suffering, and allow that understanding to turn into compassion. When compassion suffuses the mind, suffering naturally weakens, and sometimes fades away.

What Thich Nhat Hanh taught me as the Art of Suffering adds one extremely powerful tool to my toolbox for dealing with suffering: love. If there is one word that summarizes all three steps above, I think that word is *love*. Love yourself enough to allow yourself the space to suffer, without shame or judgment. In suffering, there is nothing to be ashamed of, there is no reason to hide—it's just the natural experience of the human condition, that's all. As long as we possess a human body and live a human life, there will be pain. Love yourself enough to allow the space and time to heal. Love yourself enough to cradle yourself in pain, tenderly with kindness. And love all sentient beings enough to want to cultivate compassion.

The Art of Suffering is love.

Matthieu Ricard and fellow researcher Tania Singer, while researching altruism in the brain, made a fascinating discovery. When Matthieu recollected a disturbing video of handicapped children dying from abandonment and hunger, parts of his brain associated with pain were activated. However, when he did that while he meditated on altruistic love and compassion, the cerebral networks linked to negative emotions and distress were not active, while certain cerebral areas associated with positive emotions were, for example, parts of the brain linked to feelings of affiliation and maternal love.[8] Matthieu and Tania demonstrated scientifically that altruistic love and compassion are antidotes for suffering.

I am reminded of a story I heard from the yoga master Sadhguru Jaggi Vasudev. I have not found a written source for this story, but it is a beautiful story, and I'd like to end this chapter with it. Here, it is written the way I remember hearing it from Sadhguru.

Once upon a time, there was a yogi who had been practicing vigorously for thirty years. This yogi met the great yoga master Ramakrishna and asked him, "Even after all my years of hard practice, there is something not in me that I sense is in you. What do I need to do so that what is in you is also in me?"

Ramakrishna asked, "As a yogi, have you ever loved anybody or anything?" The yogi was initially offended. "No, of course not," he said. But after much prodding by Ramakrishna, he admitted to once loving a cow many years ago. The yogi lived in the forest far away from people so he could concentrate on his practice, but he had kept a cow in his hut for the milk. After a while, our yogi started to really love the cow and became very attached to it.

One day, a wandering yogi passed by the hut and asked to stay for a few days. Our yogi welcomed him with open arms and invited him to stay for as long as he wished. But after just one day, the wandering yogi left the hut in the middle of the night without telling his host, which in Indian culture only happens when the guest is deeply offended by the host. When the host realized his guest was missing, he chased down the wandering yogi and asked why he left in such a manner. The wandering yogi said in disgust, "It is obvious that you love the cow. You are not a true yogi." Our yogi realized the visitor was right, so he gave the cow away.

When Ramakrishna heard the story, he told the yogi, "Here is what I want you to do. I want you to get a cow and take care of it for one year." The yogi did that. He learned to love the cow, this time knowing that he couldn't keep her. And a year later, he met Ramakrishna again and said to the master, "What is in you, I now also have it in me."

So my advice is: *Have* a cow, dude!

CHAPTER SEVEN

The Great Mind Is Better than Sex

An Exploration Beyond Worldly Pleasures

Once upon a time, there was a student called Peter studying theoretical physics at Cambridge University. One fateful day, Peter went on a meditation retreat, during which he managed to go very deep into his meditation and experienced the profound joy of deep meditation. He realized this joy he experienced was far more satisfying than the pleasure of sex, and he knew because he just had sex with his girlfriend about a week before the retreat. It blew him away. His first thought was, "Why didn't anybody tell me about this before?" That was when he decided to become a Buddhist monk.[1] Peter grew up to become Ajahn Brahm, one of the most prominent and respected Buddhist monks in the Western world today.

Meditation offers far more than just stress relief, mental concentration, or creativity and worldly success. As meditation practice
deepens, it opens up a vast and fascinating world, and I would love
to explore that world a little with you here. In writing the previous
chapters, I took on the role of the local native guide, showing you
the paths that I'm familiar with, not because I'm better than you in
any way, but simply because I have traveled those paths and their
shortcuts often enough that I know them well. In this chapter, I hope
to shed the role of the local native guide and speak to you as a fellow
adventurer, exploring with you the fascinating spaces that I have
only newly explored, or have scarcely traveled myself, or about which
I have only heard amazing tales from the master guides who have
traveled much farther than I have.

Let us take a short excursion into the realm of deep meditation
practices and joy beyond worldly pleasures.

Joy Is Not the Only Path

Before we explore any advanced topic on meditation, there is something we need to make clear: that the path of joy is not the only path

in developing a solid meditation practice and mental fitness. There are actually very many paths. In Buddhism, for example, there are supposed to be eighty-four thousand paths, which the Buddhists call "Dharma doors," or doors to the teachings, and behind every one of those doors is the same exact prize (which is probably why it never became a popular game show on TV).

Once again, the physical fitness analogy is instructive. To become physically fit, you can apply the easy and fun methodology we talked about, which is to find an easy way to ramp up and then make regular exercise fun. But that is obviously not the only way. You can, for example, force yourself to exercise regularly with sheer discipline. You can create the conditions for others to force you to get fit by, for example, joining the US Marine Corps. You can aim for greatness by joining an Olympic training team. Or sometimes, life circumstances force you to get fit. For example, you get a medical diagnosis that says if you don't get in shape soon, you will die, and that would be great motivation for exercise.

Similarly, in mind training, the joy methodology is a good way to progress, but not the only way. There are people who apply sheer discipline. There are people who deliberately put themselves into situations where they have no choice but to meditate. For example, when meditation master Shinzen Young was young, before he had any formal meditation training, he bought himself a one-way ticket to Japan and checked himself into a remote Buddhist monastery so he could not easily chicken out. That was his first introduction to serious meditation practice. You can also resolve to become a meditation teacher and use that as motivation for your practice. I see that a lot because my organization, the Search Inside Yourself Leadership Institute (SIYLI, pronounced as "silly," of course), trains Search Inside Yourself teachers and I insist that all of them acquire two thousand hours of meditation practice, so many of those teachers are motivated to practice in order to teach Search Inside Yourself.

Very frequently, though, people take the path of pain. For example, many people signed up for Jon Kabat-Zinn's Mindfulness-Based Stress Reduction (MBSR) class because they were in serious physical pain that their doctors couldn't do anything about, so their entire early mindfulness practice was around pain. I myself came to meditation because of my chronic and persistent emotional pain. In fact, among people of my generation or older, almost 100 percent of all meditators I know came to meditation because they were miserable. That makes sense because when I was growing up, meditation was far from mainstream, so the population that self-selected into meditation had to have very strong motivation to venture that far out, and in almost every case, that motivation was unbearable pain. I know of only a single exception. There is one person I know, the cofounder of a very successful and very famous Internet company, who came to meditation (and Buddhism) entirely "because Buddhism makes perfect sense." One person. All others were initially motivated by pain.

Another point to note is the paths are not mutually exclusive. For example, you can use ease and fun as a way to start exercising regularly, and a few years after that you decide you want to become very fit, so you take the path of rigor and discipline by joining the Olympic training team or the US Marine Corps. Similarly, your meditation practice may start on an ease and joy path, and then when you begin to get fairly good at it, you may decide you really want to switch to a more rigorous, disciplined approach. The thing about the different paths is that each has its own upsides and downsides, so they work much better for some people than others, depending on goals, inclinations, aptitudes, and life situations. For example, the ease and joy path is good at helping large numbers of ordinary people establish a solid practice, but if you are someone who wants to establish a deep practice in a small number of months, you can't beat buying a one-way ticket to Thailand and checking yourself into a Buddhist forest monastery in the middle of a thick rainforest with an enlightened, no-nonsense master. Sometimes, your life situation temporarily restricts your choice of practice. For example, my main practice is joy, but on days when I suffer emotional pain that is so strong it overwhelms my ability to bring up joy, I have no choice but to practice kindness and equanimity in pain. That, plus my wife would never let me buy a one-way ticket to Thailand to check myself into a forest monastery in the middle of a thick rainforest, so that option is off the table for me as well.

Given that there are a large number of paths (84,000?), why did I decide to write a book on meditation with joy? Why not one of the other 83,999 paths?

First, it is because the path of joy is my own main practice. I like things to be easy and joyful. Ease is good, joy is good. I'm too lazy to take the hard paths unless absolutely necessary. Those who take the hard paths are like legendary heroes riding ferocious tigers. Me?

I'd rather ride gentle, smiling unicorns with rainbows coming out of their rear ends.

Meng was just horsing around when he came up with that image.

Second, and most important, I hope to benefit the maximum number of people. Too many people tell me they want to meditate but meditation is too hard. Some find it too hard to even begin; most others find it too hard to sustain. I know it doesn't necessarily have to be hard. From my own experience practicing and teaching, I know it is possible to initiate and develop a solid practice primarily with ease and joy. I hope this approach will be beneficial to very many people.

When Meditation Becomes Effortless

Like many other seasoned meditators I have spoken to, I have experienced the long journey of my meditation practice in three distinct stages:

1. Relaxation

2. Attentional stability

3. Effortlessness

In the first stage, I learned to relax, to not struggle, and to be at ease with my breath. In the second stage, I learned to apply an immense amount of skillful effort to establish attentional stability upon that foundation of relaxation (I spoke about my experience cultivating both relaxation and attentional stability back in Chapter 3). After that, I arrived at the third stage, in an unexpected manner.

I had put so much effort into developing my attentional stability that I gained the ability to stay relaxed and keep my attention on the breath—and not miss a single breath for two hours at a stretch. I thought the momentum of my progress was unstoppable. And then, lo and behold, my practice hit a wall. For reasons I did not understand at the time, no matter how hard I tried, I could make no further progress. My serenity did not deepen, and I was unable to extend my meditative concentration beyond two hours. What to do? What to do?

By coincidence, I met with the Korean Zen master Subul Sunim. Near the end of our meeting, I told him that my practice was making no further progress, and I asked him what I should do. He gave me a very simple piece of advice, "Now, abandon effort." He then elaborated with a teaching that bears a touch of Zen poetry, "To acquire wisdom is very hard, but to abandon it is even harder. You have obviously accumulated a lot of wisdom, and your wisdom has brought you to this point, which is very good. But to advance further, you need to abandon that wisdom."

When I heard that, I knew it was precisely the teaching I needed to break out of my rut. Such Zen teachings were not unfamiliar to me. I had read about them for many years, but now suddenly I could use them. This is a good example of the right teaching at the right time. The Zen teachings surrounding abandoning wisdom and effort would have been totally useless to me at the stage when I was trying to establish attentional stability, but they are precisely the teachings I needed once I was able to do that. In Early Buddhism, the tradition of my own meditative training, the Buddha taught that there are four kinds of teachings: teachings that are truthful and useful, teachings that are untruthful but useful, teachings that are truthful but not useful, and teachings that are untruthful and not useful. The Buddha told his students to only speak the teachings that are truthful and useful. I realized that many, possibly all, of the teachings in the category of "truthful but not useful" are there entirely because of timing. For example, the teaching to abandon wisdom and effort has always been a truthful teaching, but it was totally useless to me at one stage of my practice, and then it became *the* most important teaching to me at another stage of my practice. The switch was entirely due to the timing of my progress as a practitioner. If you are learning to teach meditation, please take note—this is a very important point.

After Master Subul spoke, one of his assistants walked in with some urgent paperwork for him to attend to. I took the opportunity to meditate while I waited. I dropped into a meditative state, and then I abandoned all mental effort. Within seconds, there was a deep sense of calm, stability, and vividness. And it was effortless. A few minutes later, when the master was done with his paperwork, I opened my eyes and reported to him what had just happened, and he said to me, "Yes, this is it."

Suddenly, I saw that the biggest barrier to my progress was my effort. The very effort that had accelerated my progress was holding me back from the next stage of my growth. With attentional stability now firmly established, the next thing that needed to happen was for all mental activity to quiet down. Effort was itself gross mental activity; therefore, it had become a hindrance. Like the booster rockets on a space shuttle—without them, the shuttle cannot take off, but once the rocket fuel is spent, those very same rockets become dead weight and need to be ejected for the shuttle to go higher. And I had arrived at that stage.

Beyond attentional stability is effortlessness. By firmly establishing stability, the meditator puts the mind on track in a meditative state where it is alert, relaxed, and stable, and then he withdraws all mental effort, allowing the meditation to happen by itself. It is like a cart that's been given a strong push—it keeps rolling and we don't need to keep pushing. The meditator only reapplies effort when attentional stability wanes (and withdraws effort again soon after). With effort withdrawn, the mind glides into a deeply calm and quiet state. In the background, there is attention to the breath, but in the foreground, the attention is objectless. There is simply a thus-ness. Thus it is, thus it shall be. More important, joy becomes more prominent. The subtle (but highly sustainable) joy arising from ease that was ever present in the background now comes to the foreground. With the mind effortlessly stable, we experience joy more vividly.

When I was a novice, I had heard many meditation masters say that "meditation should be so effortless that it does itself." I had never understood what that meant, but now I did. It took me a huge amount of effort to get to that effortlessness. It reminds me of a funny saying, "It takes a very long time to be an overnight success."

Later on, my dear friend, meditation teacher Soryu Forall, told me of a beautiful parable from the Avatamsaka Sutra (Flower Ornament Scripture) that gave me the words to make sense of this development. It is the parable of a person pushing a sailboat to the ocean. Before arriving at the ocean, the sailboat is pushed with much effort, but once it reaches the ocean, pushing is useless. On the water, the sailboat is effortlessly propelled by the wind. The distance it travels on the ocean in one day is farther than it could be forced over land in a hundred years.[2]

The sailboat analogy carries two important lessons. The first is that effortlessness often needs to be preceded by deliberate effort. If we never push the sailboat to the ocean, if instead we foolishly sit in the sailboat while it is on land hoping for it to be "propelled without effort by the wind," we get nowhere. In meditation, effortlessness must be established on the foundation of attentional stability; otherwise it is really just mind wandering and a waste of your time. The second lesson is that while the effortful stage is important, its main role is to enable effortlessness. A meditator who does not understand this is like a sailor who keeps pushing the sailboat when it is already in the water, or worse, like the guy who pushes his sailboat all the way to the destination over land rather than pushing it to the water with the intent of sailing to the destination. He is wasting valuable time and effort.

I'd rather be sailing.

Putting the "Jolly" in the Jolly Roger, Cap'n?

What Is It Like to Be Very Seasoned at Meditation?

We can think of meditation as having three pillars: calm-abiding, insight, and sublime states. A stable stool must have at least three strong legs. In the same way, a well-rounded meditator must be strong in all three pillars of practice.

Calm-abiding practices are meditative practices that bring the mind to a collected state so that it becomes calm and relaxed, and at the same time, attention is concentrated and vivid. In the Pali language, the term that gets translated as "calm-abiding" is *samatha* (SAH-mah-tah). Insight practices are meditative practices that sharpen the mind so that it can perceive phenomena at very high resolution, specifically three processes: the process of emotion, the process of cognition, and the process of self. Practices that involve watching the arising, presence, and cessation of thoughts and sensory experiences are insight practices. The term that gets translated from Pali as "insight" is *vipassana* (vee-PAH-sa-na). Sublime states, or *brahmavihara* (BRAH-ma-vih-ha-ra), are loving-kindness, compassion, altruistic joy, and equanimity, the four states we explored in Chapter 5. All three pillars are covered by the practices in this book, for example, Settling the Mind (Chapter 3) trains samatha (calm-abiding), Noticing Joy (Chapter 4), and Just Note Gone (Chapter 4) train vipassana (insight), and all the practices in Chapter 5 train brahmavihara (sublime states).

That leads us to two questions: What is it like having a mature practice for each pillar? And what is mastery like?

Maturity of Samatha (Calm-Abiding) Practice

When your samatha practice reaches maturity, in formal meditation, in a quiet room, when nothing particularly bad is happening in your life—for example, you have not just been fired from your job, you didn't just lose your entire life savings in commodity futures, and you're not in the middle of a nasty divorce—you can bring the mind to a deep state of calmness between 95 and 100 percent of the time. In that state of mind, four qualities become very strong: relaxation, joy, attentional stability, and perceptual vividness. The mind is joyfully relaxed, not holding on to anything, yet attention on the chosen object (such as the breath) is stable, and perception is vivid because the mind is not drowsy. It is a quality of concentration that is relaxed, easy, open, and almost effortless. You can maintain this state for at least one hour at a stretch without difficulty.

With a mature samatha practice in difficult situations in real life—when things are falling apart, people are shouting at you, or you have just been fired—you are able to calm the mind a majority of the time, and the mind is able to maintain some meaningful degree of calmness, relaxation, and stability, even some joy, right in the middle of a shit storm. Maybe not all of the time, but more than half the time.

Mastery of Samatha (Calm-Abiding)

I have not gained mastery of samatha myself, but according to the ancient texts, and also according to many meditation teachers I personally know, one who masters samatha can reach those profound states of meditative concentration called the *jhanas,* where the mind reaches perfection in directing and stabilizing attention, in invoking joy (specifically, in energetic joy and gentle joy, or piti and sukha), and in concentrative one-pointedness (unification of mind with object). One teacher described the jhanas to me as states where the mind, totally enveloped in joy, can stay perfectly still, concentrating perfectly on the chosen object without any wavering of attention or any distracting thought arising, for at least four hours at a stretch, and emerge from those four hours of intense concentration feeling rested and ready for "real work."

I know of only one neurological study where the brain of a very experienced meditator was scanned while he was in various stages of jhana, and it is fascinating.[3] The most interesting part, to me, is the research team's attempt to study the component of profound joy in jhana. They did this by measuring the activation of the dopamine reward system in the brain, and yes, the research paper does describe it as "better than sexual orgasm." One key question is, if jhana is indeed more pleasurable than sexual orgasm, does it then put the dopamine reward system into overdrive? And if so, isn't it like drug abuse (or, in more technical parlance, "drug-induced hyperstimulation of the dopamine pathways")? The study revealed something surprising. According to the brain data, the activation of the reward system in jhana was actually fairly small. However, cortical activity in the brain was reduced; therefore, a much smaller reward signal could be detected and perceived as more intense. In other words, in jhana, there is only a small activation of the brain's reward system, but the brain is so quiet, it experiences that small activation as an intense amount of joy. I find this fascinating because generations of meditation teachers have taught that the mind abiding in calmness is a joyful mind, and this study may have revealed the neurological mechanism behind it. Wow.

Maturity of Vipassana (Insight) Practice

When your vipassana practice reaches maturity, in formal meditation, you have high-resolution perception of sensory data. Specifically, you have the ability to perceive the rising and passing of minute sensory phenomena more than once per second. A key measurable indicator of maturity of vipassana practice is strong heartbeat interoception, which means the ability to feel your own heartbeat in the body as and when you want to. This ability is highly correlated with robust activity in the part of the brain known as the insula, which is also highly correlated with self-awareness and empathy.[4]

When you have a mature vipassana practice in daily life, you never completely lose your mindfulness, even in difficult situations. For example, even when you are so completely triggered that you lose control of your emotion, you never completely lose the mindfulness of watching things clearly as they happen, almost as a third person. You never completely lose touch with the insights: "My thoughts are not me—they are merely thoughts. And my emotions are not me—they are merely emotions."

One of the most important markers of maturity in vipassana practice in combination with maturity in samatha practice is equanimity in the face of pain, especially mental and emotional pain. Every sensory event follows the same pattern: it begins with contact between sense organ and object, followed by the arising of sensation, then perception, and usually followed by clinging or aversion. Clinging is when the mind desperately holds on to a pleasant experience, wishing it would never end, and aversion is when the mind desperately holds back an unpleasant experience, wishing it would end right now. Every thought follows a similar pattern too: first there is conception of the thought, followed by an emotional response, followed, usually, by clinging or aversion. As we saw in Chapter 6, the direct cause of suffering is the clinging or aversion, not the sensation or the thought. Therefore, the more the mind can experience a sensory event or a thought without clinging or aversion, the less suffering it experiences. With a mature vipassana practice, you can perceive the entire chain from contact or conception to clinging or aversion, see the clinging and aversion as the direct cause of suffering, and, if you also have a mature samatha (calm-abiding) practice, you can maintain equanimity, a state without clinging or aversion, thus creating the possibility of experiencing pain without suffering or at least with less suffering. In this way, maturity in both calm-abiding and insight creates the conditions for the blossoming of equanimity. The stronger one is in samatha and vipassana, the more one can remain calm, even, and free in the face of eight worldly conditions: gain and loss, honor and dishonor, praise and blame, and pleasure and pain.

My friend and Tibetan Buddhist master the Fourth Trungram Gyaltrul Rinpoche, who is also the first Tibetan lama reincarnate to earn a PhD from Harvard University, offered me what I think is the best technical description of a mature vipassana practice from a traditional perspective. He bases his description on the Buddhist concept of *nama-rupa* (literally: "name and form"), which refers to two processes of experience. *Nama* (literally: "name") refers to the mental aspect of experience, while *rupa* (literally: "form") refers to the physical aspect of experience. Gyaltrul tells me that in Tibetan Buddhism, nama-rupa is seen on two dimensions, nama on the y-axis and rupa on the x-axis. Rupa is the spatial dimension—all of rupa is contained in space. Nama is the temporal dimension—all of nama is in past, present, and future. The practice concerning nama is to keep trying to slice off past and future (the top and bottom parts of the y-axis) from experience until nama becomes very thin, while the practice concerning rupa is to keep expanding it until it covers all the space that can be perceived by the senses. That is, to focus your experience on the present instead of the past or future, and to broaden your experience of the present until it includes everything that is happening.

I found this framing to be very useful for my own practice. When I tried it out, I had a sudden change in perception. Initially, the breath was perceived as breath, and bodily sensations were perceived as sensations in the body. But when the experiencing of nama got to be sufficiently thin, there was a phase shift. Suddenly, the mind experienced sensations as a cacophony of micro events. A sudden tingling here, a tingling there, a sound here, a vibration there, an expansion here, a contraction there. There was so much input, so noisy. And then it occurred to me that even the breath itself is a concept, a concept made up of many successive moments of sensation that the mind integrates as the experience of breath. I also saw that the number of phenomena noticed by mind goes up substantially from about one per second to about ten per second. And then I realized, one of the marks of a mature vipassana practice is the ability to effortlessly switch between the two levels of perception, the conceptual level in which we normally operate (things, people, actions) and the preconceptual level before the mind integrates sensory data and thought streams into operational concepts. In other words, the ability to see things in more than one way. This is territory I'm newly exploring myself.

Is this because you meditated after watching *Inception*?

Mastery of Vipassana (Insight)

I have not reached the mastery of vipassana myself, so this is territory I know of only from what the masters have taught me. As far as

I know, there is no consensus on what constitutes mastery of vipassana, but I'm fairly sure I know the bare minimum qualification, what meditation master Shinzen Young described to me as "the realization that there has never been such a *thing* called a self within me." Shinzen also helpfully explained that different people perceive this realization differently, depending largely on their spiritual tradition. Buddhists, for example, tend to experience it as an absence of self. Taoists tend to speak of it as oneness with all things, whereas contemplatives in the Abrahamic religions (Judaism, Christianity, Islam) tend to formulate it as the union of the soul with God. In all cases, the common point is the disappearance of the sense of the small, immutable, and bounded "self." I have heard that same state described by other masters as "realization leading to the complete breaking of identification with one's mind and body" and also as "the realization that there is no boundary or separation between 'self' and others at all." It is actually very hard to describe this state because it is not a common daily experience, so please treat every description as a poor approximation. Ancient teachings compare the verbal description of profound meditative realizations to describing the taste of honey to someone who has never tasted sweetness in his life, so all such descriptions are necessarily unsatisfactory.

In Pali, the above point of realization is labeled *sotapatti* (literally: "entering the stream") and in Japanese, it is labeled *kensho* (literally: "seeing [true] nature") or *satori* (literally: "understanding," usually translated as "awakening"). Shinzen compares it to the paradigm shifts that occur periodically in the history of science. For example, take the realization that lunar eclipses are caused by the shadow of the earth being cast on the moon: once you gain that realization, you will never again believe (as old Chinese customs do) that lunar eclipses happen when the Heavenly Dog tries to eat the moon again, and therefore you never again desire to make loud noises to scare away the Heavenly Dog (as my grandparents used to do). A paradigm shift in science permanently changes the way we view certain aspects of reality and, therefore, changes our mental states and behaviors. In the same way, the realization that there has never been such an immutable object called a self permanently changes the way you perceive your own personhood. From then on, you will only see self as a process, not an object. Extending the metaphor regarding lunar eclipse—the eclipse still happens and it still looks like a monster eating the moon, but you no longer interpret it as such. After stream entry, mental images, mental talk, and emotional body sensations still arise just like before, but they are no longer interpreted as a thing called self.

That has obvious implications for suffering. A large percentage of our suffering comes from the sense of I, myself, and mine, all of which originate from the sense of a solid, substantial self, so once the sense of self is realized to be a process that is completely mind-generated, then a lot of suffering either goes away or is greatly reduced. I asked Soryu Forall, how much does sotapatti reduce suffering? Soryu said he was unable to quantify it, but he told me an ancient text says that before sotapatti, the volume of suffering is like an ocean, and after sotapatti, it is reduced to a teardrop. Holy moly.

As a fellow adventurer, I can share with you a description of the tiny bit of territory I have personally explored on this subject of nonself. It is nowhere near what the masters have described, but since my exploration is much closer to our day-to-day worldly experience, it may be helpful to you. In my exploration, I learned that there are at least two flavors of nonself, one weaker and one stronger. The weaker flavor is the experience that **there is only the observer, and the observer has no identity.** This flavor is actually quite easy to describe and fairly straightforward for someone with strong samatha and vipassana practice to arrive at. When we sleep, we sometimes dream.

In our dreams, we are sometimes an entirely different person from the person in real life. In other words, in those dreams, we have an entirely different identity as the person who is awake. During the process of falling asleep and getting into that dream, the mind abandons one identity and takes on another. My experience of the first flavor of nonself took that path. Once, as I was in deep meditation, the mind became subtle enough to enter that dreamlike state while being vividly aware, and it arrived at the state after the mind abandons one identity but before the mind takes up another. In that state, there was only the observer, and the observer had no identity whatsoever. There was no "Meng," that "Meng" completely disappeared. There was only the observer. I was able to stay in that state for roughly thirty minutes, and that experience was life changing. In my life, some large percentage of my suffering arises from issues involving my identity ("How dare they treat *me* like this? Who do they take *me* for?" "Why am *I* not lovable?" "Why does he treat *me* like *I* am incompetent?") When the observer has no identity, the observer gains experiential realization that **identity is entirely mind-made.** Identity has no substance whatsoever—it is nothing but a mere creation of mind.

I think, therefore I'm Meng.

I think your usual meditation posture is comfier.

Having experienced that realization, when one gets back to real life, identity-related problems such as being treated like I'm useless or unimportant still sting, but the mind also knows that there is zero substance to that identity anyway, so the suffering is meaningfully reduced.

The stronger flavor of nonself that I experienced is **there is no observer—there is only the observation.** This is currently exploratory territory to me (which means yes, there may be another book coming from me in a few years, thank you for asking). I have only experienced it a few times myself, and I have not yet developed the ability to stabilize it. The first time I experienced this flavor of nonself was when I was attending intensely to sound. I was told it is for precisely this reason that some Zen masters consider sound to be the king of meditation objects. The advantage of meditating on sound is, unlike the breath or the body, the mind does not perceive sound as an embodied experience. Instead, it perceives sound as an experience "outside." Because of this lack of embodiment, it is much easier to experience sound without the observer arising in response to the experience. In this flavor of the nonself experience, the mind observes the sound but does not experience the presence of an observer, and then one moment later, the mind constructs the observer to cognize the absence of the observer in the previous moment. I know, this may not make much sense to you. At this point, all I know is my meditation teachers tell me that this ability to experience the absence of the observer, when I cultivate and stabilize it and learn to turn it on or off at will, leads eventually to sotapatti. I'll report back to you when I learn more (except the version of "I" doing the reporting will be an observer with an identity, sorry).

Maturity of Brahmavihara (Sublime States) Practice

When your brahmavihara practice reaches maturity, you can, in formal meditation, bring up loving-kindness, compassion, or altruistic joy on demand, and you are able to maintain it for the duration of a fairly long sit. In daily life, in a normal setting where nobody is shouting at you or treating you badly, you can feel loving-kindness toward 95 to 100 percent of every human being you see. Even in a difficult situation, when someone is hurting you badly, you can see this person with some kindness and compassion. You can see his suffering, and you can see how his suffering causes his unskillful behavior. Because you are able to do that, some meaningfully large percentage of the time, you are able to use loving-kindness and compassion to resolve difficult situations.

It is important to understand that even if you are able to deal with every single difficult situation using loving-kindness and compassion, it does not guarantee that you will be successful in resolving every difficult situation 100 percent of the time. What loving-kindness and compassion do is increase the probability of successful resolution, and that increase is often meaningful enough to be life changing. A good analogy is the batting average. In baseball, the batting average is defined as the number of hits divided by at bats, which basically means the percentage of time that a batter hits the ball when he is supposed to. In a major league season, the batting average is somewhere around .260 (it was .268 in 2007 and .251 in 2014), which means that a Major League Baseball player hits the ball about 26 percent of the time. Typically, a season batting average higher than .300, which is roughly 4 percentage points above the average, is considered to be excellent. The career batting average of Babe Ruth, perhaps the greatest player of all time, is .342. So the difference between Babe Ruth and the average major league player is only about 8 percentage points. The first insight learned here is that even Babe Ruth doesn't hit the ball all the time—in fact, only a minority of the time. Second, the difference between the average and what is considered excellent is a mere 4 percentage points. It is the same with loving-kindness and compassion practice as applied to real life. It doesn't mean every situation of conflict with your spouse, your in-laws, your boss, or your customers will be resolvable with loving-kindness and compassion. For example, even if you treat your boss kindly, it doesn't mean that she will always reciprocate in kind (no pun intended) and everything will be handy and dandy. However, loving-kindness and compassion increase the probability of making a situation better, and sometimes, even a small increase in probability could have life-changing consequences. For example, the one time it makes a difference could be the one time your future parents-in-law feel so touched by your kindness, they decide you are worthy of their daughter, and that could affect the rest of your life. It is important to know about this so that you will not be discouraged that loving-kindness and compassion do not work in every situation. In the long term, practicing loving-kindness and compassion will change you and your life for the better.

Mastery of Brahmavihara (Sublime States)

I can say for certain that I am nowhere near achieving mastery in any of the four sublime states. Fortunately, I know of great people who have, so I can tell you their stories.

In formal meditation, one indicator of mastery in the sublime states is the ability to use them as vehicles to reaching jhana (that state of perfectly stabilized attention, concentration, and joy). Ajahn Brahm, for example, told me that it is possible to bring up loving-kindness in the mind to such a high intensity that the mind becomes totally collected onto it, and the mind becomes sufficiently collected to go into jhana. Another indicator of mastery is the ability to create off-the-charts changes in the brain while meditating on a sublime state, as Matthieu Ricard can do while meditating on compassion.

Where the mastery of brahmavihara really shines is in real life. I can tell you of two awe-inspiring stories that dropped my jaw. The first story was told by the Dalai Lama. He tells of a Tibetan monk, a high lama, who was thrown in jail by the secret police for decades and frequently tortured. He was eventually let out, and he found his way to India to meet the Dalai Lama. The Dalai Lama asked the monk how he felt when he was being tortured, and the monk said he was often in great danger. "What kind of danger?" the Dalai Lama asked. The monk answered, "I was in danger of losing compassion

for my torturers." I was floored when I heard that story. I mean, that guy was getting tortured, and he was worried about losing compassion for the people torturing him. Whoa.

The second story concerns a saintly small man called A. T. Ariyaratne, known affectionately to all his friends as Dr. Ari. Dr. Ari is a high school English teacher best known for founding the Sarvodaya Shramadana Movement in Sri Lanka. It started when he took forty high school students and twelve teachers from his school to an outcaste village to help the villagers fix it up, and it grew into the biggest nongovernmental organization in Sri Lanka benefiting eleven million people and fifteen thousand villages. Brahmavihara is one of the main guiding principles of the Sarvodaya organization.

In the 1960s when Dr. Ari was still a schoolteacher, a day before he was to launch a *satyagraha* (a nonviolent resistance campaign) with hundreds of students, he received news that the notorious underworld boss called Choppe was planning to assassinate him with a bomb the next day. Dr. Ari went to the home of Choppe with a fellow teacher. He first spoke with Choppe and inquired what they were planning to do the next day. Then he revealed his identity and asked Choppe to kill him then and there. He said, "Ours is a Buddhist school. Do not desecrate that sacred Buddhist seat. If you want to kill me, kill me here and now." Choppe cried and said, "If I had had teachers like you, I would never have become an underworld boss." He ordered his gang to cancel the bombing next day. Choppe and Dr. Ari became the best of friends.

Oh, if you are not tired of inspiring stories, I have one more for you. Vishnu Vasu, my friend, a documentary maker, and a longtime friend of Dr. Ari, told me that the courage of compassion runs in Dr. Ari's family. He told me this amazing story, which happened during the civil war in Sri Lanka, where ethnic Sinhalese and ethnic Tamils went to war against each other. In 1983, there were brutal riots against the minority Tamils. Dr. Ari (himself a Sinhalese) hid a group of Tamils in his house to protect them from a rampaging Sinhalese mob. The mob found out and knocked on the door of Dr. Ari's house. Dr. Ari and his wife were away (they were actually at the main campus of Sarvodaya, where they were also hiding a large number of Tamils). Dr. Ari's daughter, Sadeeva, then a young woman, opened the door. The mob asked Sadeeva to surrender the Tamils. Sadeeva said, "My father is not here, but I know if you were to ask him, he would say, 'You have to kill me first.' My mother is not here, but I know if you were to ask her, she would say, 'You have to kill me first.' And so, I'm telling you now, you have to kill me first." The mob left.

Strive Hard to Let Go

In striving toward mastery in samatha, vipassana, and brahma-vihara—calm-abiding, insight, and sublime states—what are we trying to achieve? Well, we are not trying to achieve anything at all. It is very important to understand that ultimately, meditation is not about getting anything—**meditation is entirely about letting go.** In fact, I can summarize my entire twenty-plus years of meditation practice in just two words: letting go. The *entirety* of my practice is learning to let go. For example, early on, I learned to let go of my addiction to constant sensory and mental stimulation. A bit later on, I learned to let go of restlessness and distraction during sitting meditation. Much later on, I learned to let go of some amount of greed, hatred, anxiety, and destructive ego. And at the current stage of my practice, I'm learning to let go of clinging, aversion, ill will, my dependence on sensory pleasure in general, and my need to fluff up my identity and ego. The entire process is nothing but letting go.

At every stage of letting go, I was rewarded with a new source of wholesome joy. For example, when I let go of the need to constantly be stimulated by some sensory pleasure, I experienced the joy of ease. I developed the ability to be joyful simply by sitting down and relaxing. When I let go of some meaningful amount of anger and resentment, I experienced the joy of goodwill. When I let go of my compulsion to not feel the unpleasant feelings relating to my failure, I experienced the joy of confidence. In every single case, what I experienced was the **joy of freedom,** for example, the joy of freedom from boredom, freedom from want, freedom from anxiety, freedom from my own ego, and freedom from resentment. I am, and have always been, enslaved by two tyrannical masters: my clinging to sensory and ego pleasures, and my aversion to all things unpleasant to senses and ego. I am the slave of Clinging Monster and Aversion Monster. With every bit more of letting go, I gain a little bit more freedom from this enslavement. In freedom, there is great joy.

But wait, if it is simply about letting go, isn't it easy? One thing I hear a lot from some meditation teachers I know, which used to annoy me to no end, is their teaching that letting go should be easy. A person suffering from greed, hatred, anxiety, fear, lust, or any other afflictive mental state is like she is holding a piece of burning hot coal in her hand. The solution? Just open the hand and let go of the hot coal. In the same way, simply let go of greed, hatred, anxiety, fear, lust, or anything else. Easy, right?

No, it is not easy, dammit! Well, at least not for me. The reason it is not easy is because there are **prerequisite abilities to letting go.** In the case of the person holding the piece of burning hot coal, for example, in order to let go of the hot coal, she needs the ability to open her hand. That is the prerequisite ability for that situation. If, for example, her hand is cramped, or she is suffering from some form of serious neurological condition, or her hand is paralyzed by a poisonous snakebite, she will be unable to open her hand, and she will not be able to let go of the coal. Hence, letting go is easy *only* in the presence of the right prerequisite abilities.

That is why my journey of letting go requires so much effort and practice—all the effort and practice goes into developing the prerequisite abilities for letting go. For example, all that training in mindfulness is to strengthen the prefrontal cortex of my brain so that I can develop the ability to let go of distractions. All that training in samatha (calm-abiding) and vipassana (insight) is so I can develop the ability to let go of addiction to sensory desire. All that training in brahmavihara (sublime states) is so I can develop the ability to let go of ill will. In every case, there are two parts: the immense effort to develop the prerequisite abilities for letting go, and the letting go itself. There has to be *both* effort and letting go. Ajahn Brahm has a funny analogy involving a donkey in his wonderful book *Mindfulness, Bliss, and Beyond.* Here it is (edited for length):

> *[In the old days, when people used donkeys to pull carts, they] would attach a long stick to the cart, so that it extended a couple of feet in front of the donkey's head. A string was tied to the front end of the stick, and a big juicy carrot tied to the end*

of the string. Motivated by . . . the carrot . . . , the donkey would
move forward and thereby pull the cart. . . . Buddhist donkeys,
however, know how to get that carrot! They run like hell after
that carrot, putting maximum effort (viriya) and concentration
(samadhi) into moving that cart as fast as they can. Of course,
the carrot moves just as fast, always remaining a couple feet
in front of the donkey's mouth. At this point, the Buddhist
donkey . . . suddenly [stops]! Because of momentum, the carrot
swings even further from the donkey, arcing up further than
it has ever been before. But this donkey has faith (saddha)
and wisdom (panna) and so waits patiently with mindfulness
(sati), since effort and concentration have done their work.
Patiently observing, the donkey sees the carrot swing away to
the extreme, and then sees it begin to swing back again. . . .
Practicing patience, the donkey does nothing. It is the carrot
that does all the work as it comes closer and closer. At the right
moment, the donkey simply opens its mouth and the big juicy
carrot comes in all by itself. Crunch! Munch! Mmm! [5]

Freedom!

One of the most fascinating meditation texts I have come across is a
set of instructions written for a cook. It was written in the year 1237
by the Zen master Dogen Zenji (1200–1253), founder of Soto Zen
in Japan and one of the greatest Zen masters in Japanese history.
The title of the text is *Tenzo Kyokun,* which literally means "instructions for the monk in charge of cooking meals" (usually rendered in
English as *Instructions for the Cook*). True to the Zen teaching that
meditation practice happens both on the meditation cushion and

in all activities in daily life, the *Tenzo Kyokun* mixes mundane instructions such as "When that day's gruel is finished, wash the pots, steam the rice, and prepare the soup" with some profound meditation instructions. To me, the most important instruction in the text is Dogen's instruction to practice the Three Minds: The Joyful Mind, the Caring Mind, and the Great Mind.

I learned of Dogen's Three Minds about a quarter of the way through the writing of this book, and to my pleasant surprise, I realized it corresponds directly to what I had planned to write about, in exactly the same order taught by Dogen. First, we establish the Joyful Mind, both in meditation and in daily life. In addition to joy, establish the Caring Mind. I found it very interesting that Dogen's words that got translated as "caring mind" in English literally mean "old mind" in the original Japanese. Dogen explained that the old mind is "the spirit of fathers and mothers"—it is the mind of a loving parent caring for his or her beloved only child. In other words, it is the mind of loving-kindness, compassion, and altruistic joy. Finally, on top of the Joyful Mind and the Caring Mind, we establish the Great Mind.

What is the Great Mind? The Great Mind is the mind of freedom. The Great Mind described by Dogen in the *Tenzo Kyokun* is beyond the scope of this book (specifically, Dogen talked about mind of nonduality, and I joke that I get nonduality only half the time), but there is one extremely important aspect of that freedom that is within the scope of this book, and that is **freedom from the causes of suffering**.

Ultimately, the reason to practice and master meditation is to free ourselves and others from all suffering and its causes. It is not about stress relief, or creativity, or confidence; it is not even about enjoying food better. It is about reducing, perhaps even eliminating, suffering in the world, beginning with reducing or eliminating suffering within oneself, and to start by cultivating inner peace, inner joy, and compassion. Peace is the beginning of the end of all suffering.

My friends, I hope you will become strong in all three pillars of your practice—samatha, vipassana, and brahmavihara—and master at least one of them, and in doing so, I hope that you will embody inner peace, inner joy, and compassion, and thereby reduce or eliminate the suffering in this world.

Don't Stop and Don't Strain

When I started writing my first book, *Search Inside Yourself,* I wasn't intending to write a book at all—I was just writing down notes. Back in 2007, when I was still an engineer at Google, I led the creation of the mindfulness-based emotional intelligence curriculum there called Search Inside Yourself. It quickly became the highest-rated course in all of Google (and remains so to this day, on the day I'm writing this sentence, which is Friday, in case you ask). In 2010, I decided we needed to train more teachers for the course, so I started writing down in detail what I taught in class, to serve as teaching notes for future teachers. It quickly dawned on me that I was actually writing a book, so I decided to turn it into a book project. I asked my manager at Google, Karen May, for thirteen weeks of unpaid leave to write the book. Karen looked at me with her usual kindness and concern that she appears to have an unlimited supply of, and asked,

"Do you realistically think you can write an entire book in thirteen weeks?" I said, "I have no idea, but I know one way to find out." My leave request was approved.

Karen was right—I wasn't able to write the book in thirteen weeks. It took me fourteen weeks. I had a good explanation for Karen, though. During my writing period, the Dalai Lama was in town for almost a week, and I spent most of that time with him. The Dalai Lama has become my excuse for tardiness.

Writing my second book, the book you are reading right now, has been an entirely different experience. My literary agent, Stephanie, warned me that writing a second book is usually much harder than writing a first one. The reason: by the time you get down to writing your first book, the content has probably been in your head for a very long time, whereas in writing your second book, you don't usually have the same luxury. She was right. My experience writing this book is one that appears more typical for an author: prolonged and very stressful. Writing spread over nine months, involving hundreds of hours of intense writing, researching, reviewing, and editing, and I did that while holding a day job and dealing with a multitude of other issues in my life. When I was done, I promised myself *never* again to write another book while holding a day job, ever. Some author friends tell me writing a book is like being pregnant: near the end of the process, you vow never to do it again, and then you change your mind after a few months or years.

Through the very stressful process of writing this book, I had plenty of opportunities to practice what I preach here, including easing into joy, inclining the mind toward joy, and uplifting the mind with joy in the midst of difficulty, all of which worked. In addition, throughout the whole process, I realized I was practicing a principle that applies not just to writing this book but also to every long and difficult endeavor, including most of life itself. It may even be the case that this one principle underlies everything I have written about in this book, and the principle is: Don't Stop and Don't Strain.

As usual, I learned this important lesson from an ancient Buddhist text. In the text, someone poetically asks the Buddha how he attained deliverance: "How, dear sir, did you cross the flood?"[1] The Buddha answers, "By not stopping, friend, and by not straining I crossed the flood." The Buddha further explains that if he had strained, he would have been swept away, and if he had stopped, he would have sunk. Therefore, he did not stop and did not strain. This is a very important lesson for me. In any kind of difficult situation, especially one that appears prolonged, I must aspire to have the determination to not give up, and also to cultivate the inner peace, inner joy, and compassion to be at ease as much as possible.

I hope this will be a useful lesson for you too. No matter where you are in life or what is happening around you—if you wake up happy or sad, if you are quick to anger or afraid to speak up, if you are trying to accomplish something and you cannot see the end—this principle, and the practices I have shared in this book, offer a more joyful way through.

My friends, on your path to inner greatness, may you never stop and never strain.

Acknowledgments

When I look back on my life, I feel I have been saved by amazing grace. I used to be so miserable my life trajectory could have taken one of many very bad directions. I could have stayed miserable for the rest of my life, and thanks to my unfortunately high intelligence, become very effective at spreading suffering around me. Or, I could have spent my whole life feeling bitter and wallowing in self-pity. Or, quite likely, I might have ended my life early (on purpose, or otherwise). But happily, none of that happened. Almost by chance, I learned that happiness is a highly trainable mental skill. I trained, and I became happy. Better than that, I became a good person (or, at least, less of a dick than I used to be). As an unintended side effect of that training, I also became successful in a worldly sense beyond my wildest dreams. Wow.

The wisdom and training methods that afforded me this dramatic change in my life trajectory come from the Buddha. In fact, all that is good in me comes from the Buddha and his teachings. I was lost, but now I'm home. Every moment in meditation where the mind is at peace, I feel I'm home. I have taken to reading the (very voluminous) collection of the original text of Early Buddhism known as the *Nikayas* (literally: volumes), and with every discourse I read I feel I am home. It's all so familiar to me. Thank you, beloved Old Man. I was lost, and you took me home. I am grateful to you, and grateful *for* you, every single day of my life. I hope that sometime before this lifetime ends, I will be worthy of being in your shadow.

I'm grateful to the many teachers and dear friends over the years who have taught me various aspects of the skill for happiness. Among them are His Holiness the Dalai Lama; His Holiness the Karmapa; the Most Reverend Archbishop Desmond Tutu; the late Godwin Samararatne; the Venerables Sangye Khadro, Ayya Tathaaloka Bhikkhuni, Bhikkhu Bodhi, Ajahn Brahm, Tenzin Priyadarshi, Trungram Gyaltrul Rinpoche, Sakyong Mipham Rinpoche, Matthieu Ricard, and Yongey Mingyur Rinpoche; Zen teachers Thich Nhat Hanh, Norman Fischer, Shinzen Young, Soryu Forall, and Joan Halifax; lay teachers Jon Kabat-Zinn, Jack Kornfield, Trudy Goodman, Shaila Catherine, S. N. Goenka, A. T. Ariyaratne, Thupten Jinpa, Alan Wallace, and Sharon Salzberg; yoga master Sadhguru Jaggi Vasudev; and Christian teachers Father Laurence Freeman and Brother David Steindl-Rast. Some of you may be surprised to see non-Buddhist teachers on this list. You shouldn't be. I find that the deeper one's meditative practice, the more one finds that all contemplative traditions point to the same common core of inner goodness. The Dalai Lama, for example, said that the Sermon on the Mount is very close to Buddhist thinking on nonviolence, and cause and effect. When I'm discussing the intricacies of samatha and compassion practices with Brother David, it feels no different from having the same discussion with a Buddhist master. Brother David told me his Benedictine monastery once hosted a Zen monk for several months, and at the end of his stay, all the Benedictine monks said they felt the Zen monk to be "one of us, a real brother," and the Zen monk felt the same way about the Benedictine monks. You arrive at the same beautiful place, whatever your spiritual tradition.

Thank you, dear friends and teachers, for teaching me to be happy.

I'd like to thank the very many people who have worked with me on this book. You might think that becoming a successful author is a solitary achievement. *Noooooooo....* Like everything else, the success of an author is the result of the hard work of very many people: the illustrator, the agent, the editors, the sales and marketing folks, the people who design the cover and layout, the lady who operates the printing machine, the guy who drives the delivery truck, etc., etc. Nobody succeeds on his own. Everybody who succeeds does so on the effort of other people. Thank you all, my friends. I'd especially like to mention a few people. First, Colin Goh, my extremely talented illustrator, friend, and advisor, who, once again, did an amazing job creating the cartoons for me. I'm very grateful to my agent, Stephanie Tade. Stephanie was the one who con . . . er . . . convinced me to write this book. She had much more faith in me than I had in myself. She was my guide and cheerleader at every step of the process, and she was protective of me like a caring big sister. She was, and still is, always looking out for me. All that, and she has taken the Bodhisattva Vow. I honesty could not have chosen a better book agent in the whole world, like really. (Your Holiness, if you're reading this and you're in need of a book agent, <wink> <wink> <nudge> <nudge>). I'm also very grateful for my editor, Gideon Weil. Gideon is brilliant, insightful, responsive, and caring. He is honest yet skillful, respectful, and open-minded in expressing his opinions. Dealing with authors must not be easy, and he does it with compassionate finesse. In fact, when Stephanie and I were planning this book, I decided that the only editor I wanted to work with was Gideon. That's how much I love working with him. I'd also like to thank my development editor Stephanie Higgs, my research assistant Maaheem Akhtar, my executive assistant Karen Ellis, and all the wonderful folks at HarperCollins: Melinda Mullin, Mark Tauber, Laina Adler, Hilary Lawson, Kim Dayman, Terri Leonard, Sarah Woodruff, Lisa Zuniga, Ralph Fowler, and Ali Shaw. I am thankful to friends who took the time to read through my early drafts and gave me many useful suggestions and encouragement, including Jungeun You, Richard Davidson, Matthieu Ricard, Ayya Tathaaloka Bhikkhuni, Yunha Kim, Shinzen Young, Greg Simpson, Jonathan Berent, Paul Singerman, David Yeung, Marc Lesser, Dawn Engle, Dekila Chungyalpa, Treena Huang, Vishnu Vasu, HueAnh Nguyen, Rich Hua, Catarina Ahlvik, Eric Harr, Peter Weng, and Soryu Forall. I'm also grateful to the wonderful lady, health and fitness coach Joyell Hayes (see: joyellhayes.com), for so kindly selling me the joyondemand.com domain.

I'm blessed to have many famous friends. They are all extremely busy, I know, so when I asked them for an endorsement for this book, I expected half of them to say no. However, almost all of them said yes immediately. Wow. Rather than listing them all out right here, you can find their names in the endorsements section of this book. Thank you all, my dear, wonderful friends. There is one person in particular I want to single out because his kindness and generosity moved me to tears. President Jimmy Carter. After I sent my endorsement request to President Carter, his staff informed me that he was unable to get back to me because he had just lost a twenty-eight-year-old grandson, who had died suddenly of a heart attack. I felt really sad and decided not to follow up on my request. I figured that President Carter had plenty to deal with in his life. It turned out, President Carter didn't forget my request at all. A few weeks after I asked, he surprised me by sending me a very kind endorsement for this book. I was deeply touched. I was so touched I didn't even know what to say. I could speak only in tears. With all the pain that he had to deal with, he still took the time to do something nice for me, which he totally didn't have to. Wow. I can only think of paying his kindness forward by working harder in service to the world. Thank you so much, President Carter. You are my hero.

(And yes, in case you wonder, President Carter is as kind, loving, and wonderful in person as he is in public. He inspires me to be a good person.)

I am deeply thankful to my parents. I've always known the sacrifices they made for me, including suffering physical hunger, but writing this book gave me the opportunity to reflect on their kindness even more, and I'm grateful for that. Last and foremost, I'm deeply thankful to my lovely wife, Cindy, for taking care of me and for (still) keeping me, and to my beautiful daughter, Angel, for being the greatest love of my life.

To all of you whom I owe a debt of gratitude to, let me repay you partially with this poem, mostly because it costs me nothing, and also because I did the same thing in my first book and nobody complained.

Let's go, vamanos.
Beyond the limited mind.
Everybody let's go.
Welcome to awakening!

(In original Sanskrit: *Gate, gate. Paragate.*
Parasamgate. Bodhi svaha!)

Notes

Introduction: How I Learned to Be Jolly for Fun and Profit

1. Steve Lohr, "Hey, Who's He? With Gwyneth? The Google Guy," *New York Times*, September 1, 2007, http://joyondemand.com/r/meng_nyt.

2. Chade-Meng Tan, "Everyday Compassion at Google," TED Talk, November 2010, http://joyondemand.com/r/meng_ted.

3. Anderson Cooper interviewing Chade-Meng Tan, "Mindfulness," *60 Minutes,* CBS News, December 14, 2014.

4. David G. Allan, "Google's Algorithm for Happiness," CNN, 2015, http://joyondemand.com/r/google_happiness.

5. Philip Brickman, Dan Coates, and Ronnie Janoff-Bulman, "Lottery Winners and Accident Victims: Is Happiness Relative?" *Journal of Personality and Social Psychology* 36, no. 8 (1978): 917–27.

6. David Lykken and Auke Tellegen, "Happiness Is a Stochastic Phenomenon," *Psychological Science* 7, no. 3 (1996): 186–89.

7. J. A. Brefczynski-Lewis, et al., "Neural Correlates of Attentional Expertise in Long-Term Meditation Practitioners," *Proceedings of the National Academy of Sciences of the United States of America* 104, no. 27 (2007): 11483–88.

8. Jon Kabat-Zinn, *Wherever You Go, There You Are: Mindfulness Meditation in Everyday Life* (New York: Hyperion, 1994).

9. What he taught me, I learned later on, was a form of meditation called vipassana, or insight meditation, a less rigorous version of which is popularly known in the West as mindfulness meditation.

10. Anthony Barnes, "The Happiest Man in the World?" *The Independent*, January 20, 2007, http://joyondemand.com/r/happiest_man.

11. Yongey Mingyur Rinpoche, *The Joy of Living: Unlocking the Secret and Science of Happiness* (New York: Three Rivers Press, 2008).

12. Richard Davidson, et al., "Alterations in Brain and Immune Function Produced by Mindfulness Meditation," *Psychosomatic Medicine* 65, no. 4 (2003): 564–70.

13. Matthieu Ricard, *Happiness: A Guide to Developing Life's Most Important Skill* (New York: Little, Brown and Company, 2003).

14. Shawn Achor, *The Happiness Advantage: The Seven Principles of Positive Psychology That Fuel Success and Performance at Work* (New York: Crown Business, 2010).

15. Shawn Achor, "The Happiness Dividend," *Harvard Business Review*, June 23, 2011, http://joyondemand.com/r/happiness_dividend.

Chapter One: Joy Becomes You

1. Personal communications via email.

2. Walter Isaacson, *Steve Jobs* (New York: Simon & Schuster, 2013).

3. This story, originally in Jonah Lehrer's article "The Eureka Hunt" in *The New Yorker* (July 2008), is also verified with John Kounios via personal communications.

4. Sigal G. Barsade and Donald E. Gibson, "Why Does Affect Matter in Organizations?" *Academy of Management Perspectives* 21 (February 2007): 36–59.

5. Teresa M. Amabile, et al., "Affect and Creativity at Work," *Administrative Science Quarterly* 50, no. 3 (2005): 367–403.

6. Shinzen Young, "Shinzen, the Mindful Math Geek," YouTube, December 6, 2009, http://joyondemand.com/r/shinzen_math, and personal communications.

7. Elaine Hatfield and Susan Sprecher, "Men's and Women's Preferences in Marital Partners in the United States, Russia, and Japan," *Journal of Cross-Cultural Psychology* 26, no. 6 (1995): 728–50.

8. Olivia Fox Cabane, *The Charisma Myth: How Anyone Can Master the Art and Science of Personal Magnetism* (London: Portfolio, 2013).

9. Landon Thomas Jr., "A $31 Billion Gift Between Friends," *New York Times*, June 27, 2006, http://joyondemand.com/r/billion_friends.

Chapter Two: Just One Breath? Surely You Jest

1. Y. Y. Tang, et al., "Short-Term Meditation Training Improves Attention and Self-Regulation," *Proceedings of the National Academy of Sciences of the United States of America* 104, no. 43 (2007): 17152–56.

2. Michael D. Mrazek, et al., "Mindfulness Training Improves Working Memory Capacity and GRE Performance While Reducing Mind Wandering," *Psychological Science* 24, no. 5 (2013): 776–81.

3. A. C. Hafenbrack, Z. Kinias, and S. G. Barsade, "Debiasing the Mind Through Meditation: Mindfulness and the Sunk-Cost Bias," *Psychological Science* 25, no. 2 (2014): 369–76.

4. P. Kaliman, et al., "Rapid Changes in Histone Deacetylases and Inflammatory Gene Expression in Expert Meditators," *Psychoneuroendocrinology* 40 (2014): 96–107.

5. This is a famous dialogue from the classic comedy movie *Airplane*. "Surely you can't be serious." "I am serious. And don't call me Shirley." This footnote exists for the benefit of all three of you who haven't watched that movie.

6. Michael Mosley, "The Truth About Exercise," *Horizon*, directed by Toby MacDonald, BBC Two, aired February 28, 2012.

7. Charles Duhigg, *The Power of Habit: Why We Do What We Do in Life and Business* (New York: Random House, 2012).

Chapter Three: From One Breath to One Googol

1. *Nimitta Sutta* (*The Discourse on Meditation Signs*), Anguttara Nikaya 3:103.

Chapter Four: What, Me Happy?

1. Malcolm Gladwell, "The Naked Face," *The New Yorker* (August 5, 2002).

2. *Upanisa Sutta (The Discourse on Proximate Causes)*, Samyutta Nikaya 12:23.

3. So many papers on this topic, but here is a good one, from which you can find references to many others: Kennon M. Sheldon and Sonja Lyubomirsky, "How to Increase and Sustain Positive Emotion: The Effects of Expressing Gratitude and Visualizing Best Possible Selves," *The Journal of Positive Psychology* 1, no. 2 (2006): 73–82.

4. One good paper on the power of gratitude journals is: Robert A. Emmons and Michael E. McCullough, "Counting Blessings Versus Burdens: An Experimental Investigation of Gratitude and Subjective Well-Being in Daily Life," *Journal of Personality and Social Psychology* 84, no. 2 (2003): 377–89.

5. Brigid Schulte, "To Achieve Happiness: 5 habits, 2 minutes," *The Columbus Dispatch*, July 14, 2015.

6. Akira Kasamatsu and Tomio Hirai, "An Electroencephalographic Study on the Zen Meditation (Zazen)," *Folia Psychiatrica et Neurologica Japonica* 20, no. 4 (1966): 315–36.

7. Amit Bhattacharjee and Cassie Mogilner, "Happiness from Ordinary and Extraordinary Experiences," *Journal of Consumer Research* 41, no. 1 (2014): 1–17.

8. Eric Weiner, "Bhutan's Dark Secret to Happiness," BBC, April 8, 2015, http://joyondemand.com/r/bhutan_happiness.

9. C. N. DeWall and R. F. Baumeister, "From Terror to Joy: Automatic Tuning to Positive Affective Information Following Mortality Salience," *Psychological Science* 18, no. 11 (2007): 984–90.

10. Shinzen Young, "The Power of Gone," *Tricycle*, Fall 2012.

11. Personal communications via email.

Chapter Five: Uplift the Mind in Seconds

1. Mat Smith, "Life Lessons from the World's Happiest Man," *Esquire* (December 15, 2015), http://joyondemand.com/r/matthieu_learned.

2. Nyanaponika Thera, et al., "Mudita: The Buddha's Teaching on Unselfish Joy," *Access to Insight* (2013), http://joyondemand.com/r /mudita.

3. H. H. Dalai Lama, *Beyond Religion: Ethics for a Whole World* (Boston: Mariner Books, 2012).

4. Anguttara Nikaya 5:35.

5. Barbara L. Fredrickson, et al., "Open Hearts Build Lives: Positive Emotions, Induced Through Loving-Kindness Meditation, Build Consequential Personal Resources," *Journal of Personality and Social Psychology* 95, no. 5 (2008): 1045–62.

6. In the Visuddhimagga (Path of Purification), a fifth-century Buddhist text, the near enemy of altruistic joy is puzzlingly identified as "joy based on the home life," but it basically describes unwholesome pleasure. The Visuddhimagga names the near enemies of the other three sublime states slightly less puzzlingly as greed, grief, and unknowing, respectively, which I have rendered in this section in a way that even I can understand. It is worth noting that modern meditation teachers have very similar but not usually identical lists of near and far enemies for each immeasurable. In my own case, I try to stay as close to the earliest known source as possible, which is the Visuddhimagga.

7. If you're interested to learn more, here is a short and very readable introduction to vagal tone written by James Heathers: "Introduction to Vagal Tone," http://joyondemand.com/r/vagal_tone.

8. Bethany E. Kok, et al., "How Positive Emotions Build Physical Health: Perceived Positive Social Connections Account for the Upward Spiral Between Positive Emotions and Vagal Tone," *Psychological Science* 24, no. 7 (2013): 1123–32.

9. Dacher Keltner, "The Compassionate Instinct: A Darwinian Tale of Survival of the Kindest," Meng Wu Lecture, Stanford School of Medicine, Palo Alto, CA, September 29, 2011, http://joyondemand.com/r/dacher_compassion.

10. Bethany E. Kok and Barbara L. Fredrickson, "Upward Spirals of the Heart: Autonomic Flexibility, as Indexed by Vagal Tone, Reciprocally and Prospectively Predicts Positive Emotions and Social Connectedness," *Biological Psychology* 85, no. 3 (2010): 432–36.

Chapter Six: Happiness Is Full of Crap

1. Personal communications via email.

2. Christopher Chabris and Daniel Simons, *The Invisible Gorilla: How Our Intuitions Deceive Us* (New York: Harmony, 2010).

3. Louis C. K. on *Late Night with Conan O'Brien*, NBC, October 1, 2008.

4. Thich Nhat Hanh, *The Miracle of Mindfulness* (Boston: Beacon Press, 1999).

5. Louis C. K. on *Late Night with Conan O'Brien*.

6. Personal communications.

7. Paul Reps and Nyogen Senzaki, *Zen Flesh, Zen Bones: A Collection of Zen and Pre-Zen Writings* (Boston: Tuttle Publishing, 1998).

8. Matthieu Ricard, *Altruism: The Power of Compassion to Change Yourself and the World* (New York: Little, Brown, 2015): 56–57.

Chapter Seven: The Great Mind Is Better than Sex

1. Ajahn Brahm, "Life Moments with Ajahn Brahmavamso (Ajahn Brahm)," YouTube, February 5, 2013, http://joyondemand.com/r/brahm_moments.

2. This parable is part of the seventh stage in the Ten Stages described in the Avatamsaka Sutra.

3. Michael R. Hagerty, et al., "Case Study of Ecstatic Meditation: fMRI and EEG Evidence of Self-Stimulating a Reward System," *Neural Plasticity* 2013 (2013), article ID 653572.

4. There is a collection of studies each addressing a different aspect of the relationship between emotional awareness, empathy, and the insula. Craig and Herbert suggest significant links between strong emotional awareness and awareness of inner-body feelings via activity in the insula, including perception of heartbeats, while Singer describes many studies that link the insula to empathy. Lutz suggests all these abilities are trainable with meditation.

    A. D. Craig, "Human Feelings: Why Are Some More Aware Than Others?" *Trends in Cognitive Sciences* 8, no. 6 (2004): 239–41; Beate Herbert, Olga Pollatos, and Rainer Schandry, "Interoceptive Sensitivity and Emotion Processing: An EEG Study," *International Journal of Psychophysiology* 65, no. 3 (2007): 214–27; Antione Lutz, et al., "Regulation of the Neural Circuitry of Emotion by Compassion Meditation: Effects of Meditative Expertise," *PLoS One* 3, no. 3 (2008): e1897; Tania Singer, "Understanding Others: Brain Mechanisms of Theory of Mind and Empathy" in *Neuroeconomics: Decision Making and the Brain*, 2nd ed., eds. P. W. Glimcher, et al. (London: Academic Press, 2009): 251–68.

5. Ajahn Brahm, *Mindfulness, Bliss, and Beyond: A Meditator's Handbook* (Somerville, MA: Wisdom Publications, 2006).

Epilogue: Don't Stop and Don't Strain

1. Samyutta Nikaya 1:1. The fact that this is the very first discourse in the very voluminous Samyutta Nikaya collection probably signifies its great importance. For the entire collection translated wonderfully in English, see: Bhikkhu Bodhi, *The Connected Discourses of the Buddha: A Translation of the Samyutta Nikaya*, 2nd ed. (Somerville, MA: Wisdom Publications, 2003).

ALSO BY CHADE-MENG TAN

FOREWORDS BY JON KABAT-ZINN AND DANIEL GOLEMAN

NEW YORK TIMES BESTSELLER

Search Inside Yourself

THE UNEXPECTED PATH TO ACHIEVING
SUCCESS, HAPPINESS (AND WORLD PEACE)

CHADE-MENG TAN

"Think of *Search Inside Yourself* as the Zen of Google."
—*New York Times*